ArtScroll Series®

Rabbi Nosson Scherman / Rabbi Meir Zlotowitz

General Editors

The Way

Published by
Mesorah Publications, ltd

MALIA PANZER

with PNINA LEVI

I See It

*The True and Inspiring Story of
a Young Woman's Valiant Battle
Against a Life-threatening Illness*

FIRST EDITION
First Impression … June 2002

Published and Distributed by
MESORAH PUBLICATIONS, LTD.
4401 Second Avenue / Brooklyn, N.Y 11232

Distributed in Europe by
LEHMANNS
Unit E, Viking Industrial Park
Rolling Mill Road
Jarrow, Tyne & Wear, NE32 3DP
England

Distributed in Australia and New Zealand by
GOLDS WORLDS OF JUDAICA
3-13 William Street
Balaclava, Melbourne 3183
Victoria, Australia

Distributed in Israel by
SIFRIATI / A. GITLER — BOOKS
6 Hayarkon Street
Bnei Brak 51127

Distributed in South Africa by
KOLLEL BOOKSHOP
Shop 8A Norwood Hypermarket
Norwood 2196, Johannesburg, South Africa

ARTSCROLL SERIES®
THE WAY I SEE IT
© Copyright 2002, by MESORAH PUBLICATIONS, Ltd.
4401 Second Avenue / Brooklyn, N.Y. 11232 / (718) 921-9000 / www.artscroll.com

---

Some of the names and identifying features in this true story
have been changed to maintain the privacy of the protagonists.

Book and Jacket Design: DC Design

Printed in the United States of America by Noble Book Press Corp.
Bound by Sefercraft, Quality Bookbinders, Ltd., Brooklyn N.Y. 11232

This book is dedicated
to my wonderful
Parents and In-laws
for their selfless devotion
and endless support.
All throughout,
they were my ongoing role models for
שמחת החיים and בטחון.

And of course, to my husband,
Reuven,
for everything!

And – most of all – to
הקב"ה
for helping me see it the way I did.

Malia Panzer

Table of Contents

The Way I See It

Preface

In order to write this book I have had to relive some of the most difficult and trying times of my life. Some memories came back to me in such sharp and vivid detail that it was almost as if they were happening all over again. Others were no more than vague recollections with the gaps filled in by things my family and friends told me later.

There were times of dread and terror, and there were also times of indescribable joy and relief. In good times and in bad, I remember clearly that my strong *bitachon*, my faith in Divine Providence, sustained and comforted me. For this I have to thank my family. In our home, we always lived with *bitachon*. It was in the very air I breathed as I grew up. I cannot imagine how I could have survived my ordeal without it.

When my illness struck, my family rallied around me with the most amazing outpouring of love and support. But when I would sometimes awake in the stillness of the night and face the awful reality of my condition all by myself, I knew in my heart that I was really not alone. I knew our good and loving Father in Heaven was watching over me, and I entrusted my life to Him. I am eternally grateful that He decided to let me hold on to it and watch my little children grow up.

Throughout my illness, the values my parents instilled in me kept me strong. They taught me that when Hashem tests us we are measured not only by what we do but also by how we do it. We are expected to accept our ordeals with love and humility, and to find in ourselves the courage to do the best we can. I knew that it was up to me to remain cheerful and optimistic and do everything humanly possible to cure my disease. That was the way I saw it, and I truly believe it helped me get to where I am today.

A friend called me in the hospital. After talking for ten minutes, she said, "Malia, you're unbelievable. I called to encourage you, and it turns out you're the one giving me encouragement!"

"What do you mean?" I asked, puzzled. "I'm just talking to you the way I ordinarily would."

"That's just it," she explained. "You're hooked up to the IV, stuck in the hospital for weeks, and you're talking to me so naturally! I can't believe you can be so calm."

That's when I decided to write this book.

I want to hold on to that *bitachon*. I don't want to be like another patient I heard about, who kept a diary throughout her illness and then hid it away inside a drawer and never looked at it again. I want to cherish the memory of the feeling that Hashem was looking over my shoulder every step of the way, and I want to continue to channel that feeling into my everyday life. I want to continue to have a sunny disposition, to face life with joy and look at the bright side of every situation.

I want to remember every detail and share it, with the hope that others may gain encouragement from my story.

This is the way I see it.

Blissful Times

The day I got my first inkling of my illness began like any other. In fact, it was much better than most. It was a special day, the wonderful climax to a round of holidays, festivities and celebrations that clothed our family in a mantle of pure joy for an entire month.

It was just a few days after Pesach. With half our family living in Jerusalem, this special season was the first time in months we had all been together, and it was just grand.

I am the third of six children, and we are all very close. My oldest brother Gavriel Greenberg, his wife Frieda and their two children, and my older brother David Greenberg, his wife Tova and their two children live in Jerusalem. My younger sister Rachel attends seminary there as well. My two younger brothers, Moshe and Eli, are still at home with my parents in the Flatbush section of Brooklyn. My husband Reuven Panzer and I live in the Boro Park section of Brooklyn. We have two delicious little boys, Dov and Ari. We had also considered spending the first few years of married life in Israel, but when I discovered I was pregnant just a few weeks after the wedding, we decided to stay put in our little basement apartment in Boro Park.

As you can well imagine, Pesach was one long family celebration, and indeed, it was. But as it turned out, it was far more than a family reunion. Two weeks before Pesach, smack in the middle of Pesach cleaning, my sister-in-law Tova gave birth to a beautiful baby boy. Then just days before Pesach, my sister Rachel was engaged to a wonderful boy named Levi Goldstein. The formal engagement party took place in my parents' home on Chol HaMoed. And to top everything off, on another Chol HaMoed evening we celebrated my mother's birthday. What a scene that was! I can still see my parents beaming with pride and joy as the room overflowed with children, grandchildren and pure happiness.

After the birthday party, we sat around the table and talked until very late at night just to stretch out that magical evening. Later, as Mother and I were cleaning up together in the kitchen, I said to her, "What a special time this is! *Baruch Hashem* for so many *mazel tovs!*"

"*Baruch Hashem*," Mother replied softly. "We should only know happiness. Always."

Throughout this whole month, I was incredibly busy, running back and forth between my apartment and my parents' house. I loved being in the thick of things. I enjoyed helping Mother with her Pesach cleaning while I scoured my own apartment for crumbs. All this had to be balanced with my regular responsibilities of keeping the household running smoothly so Reuven could devote his time and energy to learning in the *kollel*, sending Dov off to play group in the morning and playing with him in the afternoons, keeping Ari happy at home, baking Reuven's favorite cakes and cookies, visiting Bubbi Rothman, my mother's mother, taking the kids out for walks, doing some shopping and a thousand other things. I loved it.

Two days after Pesach, my parents invited the Goldsteins, my sister Rachel's future in-laws, for dinner, after which some of the arrangements for the wedding would be discussed. There was a sense of urgency, since Rachel would be returning shortly to Israel to complete her seminary year. Since Mother was back into her teaching schedule at Shulamith High School and also needed to take Rachel shopping, I volunteered to make a five-course dinner for twelve for the occasion.

"Are you sure?" Mother asked.

I grinned at her. "Sure. You know I've always been the cook in the family. You can't take my job away now!"

Mother laughed and gave in. And that's how I came to be standing in my mother's kitchen two days after Pesach, cooking up a storm. It wasn't easy to prepare the meal and keep an eye on the kids at the same time, but I've always thrived on challenges.

Only when everything was prepared and in the oven did I allow myself to plop down on the couch in my parents' huge living room. Little Ari, only five months old, sat on my lap. Dov, two years old, climbed onto the couch to sit beside me. I could feel it coming. Any minute, they would demand my attention.

"It's break time, kiddies," I announced out loud. I was exhausted.

It was all catching up with me. Much as I hated to admit it, I knew I would have to slow down a little. I'd been feeling tired even before Pesach, and on Chol HaMoed, I'd begun getting mild headaches. Obviously, I needed a rest. I couldn't expect to keep up this crazy schedule and nurse a five-month-old baby at the same time.

I was still sitting on the sofa holding Ari on my lap, when Mother came home from teaching.

"Hi, Malia," she called cheerfully across the hallway. She went into the dining room, dropped her pocketbook and briefcase on the table and joined me in the living room. Dov came running to his Bubbi for a hug.

"Hi," I said with extra cheerfulness, trying to conceal my exhaustion. "How was school?"

"Just fine." She sniffed appreciatively. "Everything's ready, I see. Or rather, I smell. It all smells delicious."

"I just hope it tastes as good as it smells," I said with a grin as she reached for Ari.

"Oh, I'm sure it will," Mother replied. She cuddled Ari on her lap and looked me over carefully. She frowned. "Malia, you're looking very pale. Have you eaten lunch?"

"Uh, not really. I'm not very hungry."

"Well, when did you eat breakfast?"

"I didn't."

"You didn't?"

I smiled sheepishly. "I'm not hungry, that's all."

"Well, you'd better eat something," she said decisively. She stood up. "It's 3:00 in the afternoon, and you shouldn't be fasting like this. You've been working all morning preparing a big dinner, and you're a nursing mother. You have to take care of yourself."

I followed Mother obediently into the kitchen.

She was right. I always have a robust appetite, and it was strange that I shouldn't feel hungry. It dawned on me that I'd had no appetite at all for several days. Maybe it was the constant, nagging headaches?

It's probably just the Pesach food, I reassured myself. After all that matzah and potatoes, who could even think of eating?

The hours went by quickly. Soon it was time for our guests to arrive. The dinner was a big success. Rachel was all smiles as she sat and talked to her future mother-in-law. The evening flew by as we discussed plans for the future. Rachel would go back to Israel to complete her year in seminary. The wedding would take place some time after she returned in June, in order to give us time to get everything ready. After a great deal of talk, my parents and the Goldsteins settled on a date in early September. It was very late by the time we said our last good-byes to the Goldsteins and started cleaning up.

"I'm glad Reuven and I are still staying here tonight," I yawned as I stacked dishes in the dishwasher. "I'm whacked!"

Mother laughed. "Of course you are. Malia, you do realize what's happening, don't you?"

I felt puzzled. "What do you mean?"

She smiled at me. "Malia, it's obvious. You've been pale for the last several days, you have no appetite, and you're tired. Malia, there's no other explanation. You must be expecting!"

I stared at Mother for a moment, then laughed and shook my head. "No, I'm sure I'm not."

"What other explanation could there be?" Mother said reasonably. "Do me a favor, Malia. Take a pregnancy test. Just to make sure."

"Oh, come on," I protested. "I'd know if I was pregnant."

"I know anemia when I see it," Mother insisted. "Just buy the test, all right?"

"All right," I surrendered. "But it'll just be a waste of $12."

"So waste it," Mother said, smiling. "I'll pay you back."

As I slowly climbed the stairs to my room that night, I wondered if my mother could possibly be right. It really was unusual for me to feel so tired. I'm always exercising, walking long distances and swimming for hours. And here I was out of breath after climbing just a single flight of stairs!

I discussed the idea with Reuven. "I don't think I'm expecting," I said. "But who knows? And it would make Mother feel better."

Reuven nodded. "Sure, go ahead. It can't hurt. Do you want me to pick up the test for you on the way back from *shul* tomorrow?"

"No, that's okay. I'll get it myself."

The next morning, I was up bright and early. As always, Ari and Dov made sure I didn't sleep late. I left Dov happily eating breakfast in the kitchen with his Bubbi and went to the drugstore to purchase a pregnancy test. I was back within fifteen minutes.

"Where's Reuven?" I asked as I entered the kitchen.

"He went to *shul* with Father and Eli," Mother said. "He said he would come back before he goes to kollel." She looked meaningfully at the brown paper bag in my hand. "Why don't you go take care of that so you'll have news for him when he gets back?"

"Right."

I patted Dov's cheek before turning and heading upstairs to my room to take the test in privacy.

Five minutes later, I had the results. The test was negative.

I sat on the edge of my bed for a few moments, thinking as well as I could with my now-constant headache. Last night, my mother's idea had seemed silly, but I'd almost made up my mind this morning that she was right. Now that I knew I wasn't expecting, I began to feel nervous.

What was wrong with me?

Wacky Numbers

Reuven came upstairs a few minutes later to see how I was doing. I showed him the negative results of the pregnancy test. I tried to hide the look of concern in my eyes, but he was too perceptive. You can't hide things from Reuven.

"Don't worry, Malia," he said tenderly. "You just need a good rest. You've just had a baby five months ago, and you're nursing. What do you think you are? Still a teenager? You can't run around as much as you've been lately without tiring yourself out. What do you expect?"

"I guess you're right," I said doubtfully.

"Of course I am. Husbands are always right."

I smiled at him, but I couldn't help feeling anxious. If I wasn't expecting, what was wrong with me? Why was I feeling so weak?

Mother tackled me as soon as the men had finished their breakfasts and left for the morning.

"Something's wrong, Malia," she said quietly. She is a trained and certified EMT (emergency medical technician), and she is very much attuned to medical warning signs. "There must be some reason you've been so weak and pale lately."

"I guess so," I said uneasily. "I think I'll take a couple of days off and just rest. Maybe I have some bug or something."

My mother gave me a thoughtful looked. "You ought to see a doctor."

"Oh, no," I said quickly. "I don't need a doctor. Besides, it's Friday. Who has time to go sit at the doctor's office for two hours on a Friday?"

"Well, take a blood test then. Just get a CBC (complete blood count) done. It's only a finger prick. Maybe all you need are iron pills or something."

"Fine," I said. "I'll do it."

Whom was I to call? I didn't have a general practitioner. I'd never been sick. I can't remember ever missing a day of school as a child. The only doctors I knew were my obstetrician and Dr. Shapiro, my children's pediatrician. I decided to call Dr. Shapiro, because she is usually easier to reach.

"Good morning, Malia," she said cheerfully when I got through to her office. "What's up? Is Dov being cranky?"

"No, it's nothing like that. This time it's me. I'd like to come in and have a blood test taken. Do you accommodate mothers too? You know I'm just a kid at heart."

"I'm sure you are." I could hear her turning pages. "I can squeeze you in at 1:00. Try to be here on time, okay?"

"No problem. And thanks."

Mother was clearly relieved to see me taking some kind of action. "You'll let me know what happens, won't you?" she asked as she prepared to leave for school. "I'll probably be home by the time you get back, but call me in school if there's a problem."

"I will," I promised.

I stood by the front window with Dov and Ari, waving to Bubbi as she drove away.

For the moment, I had the house to myself. My parents were both teaching. Rachel, who would be returning to Israel on Motzaei Shabbos, was getting in some last-minute shopping. Eli had gone to visit a friend. Reuven and Moshe had both gone off to learn. They would be back at lunchtime, but that was hours away.

For a few minutes, I wandered restlessly through the rooms of the house. I couldn't seem to settle down to anything. Finally, I decided to bake *challah*, which I do for my parents almost every week. I especially wanted to bake on the very first Shabbos after Pesach, when many people make *shlissel challah*, with either a key tucked away inside the *challah* or the shape of a key braided onto the top.

I found a spare key in the house and wrapped it in foil before I assembled flour, oil, yeast, eggs and the other ingredients for *challah*. I pulled the mixer down from the shelf and nearly dropped it on the counter. I stopped to catch my breath and proceeded more carefully. When the dough was ready, I covered it with a towel and set it on the counter to rise. By that time, it was 11:00 a.m.

I went to rest in the living room, where the kids were playing. Ari gurgled excitedly when he saw me, and I picked him up and squeezed him. Silently, I thanked Hashem for my precious little boys. When Dov had been born, I'd gladly quit my secretarial job for the much more important task of being a full-time mother. I wanted to be there for my children, to bring them up through example, just like my parents had done for me. But to do so I would need strength, and that seemed to be in short supply right now.

Reuven came home a little while later. The kids were delighted to see their Father. Dov rushed to him and Ari smiled.

"What's the story, Malia?" Reuven asked as he swung Dov up into the air.

"I'm going to get a blood test," I replied. "I have a one 1:00 appointment with Dr. Shapiro."

Reuven thought about it for a moment and nodded. "Sounds good to me."

"I'm glad you think so." I handed Ari to him. "Let me put together some lunch for you, and then I'll get ready to go."

When I went into the kitchen, I saw that the dough had already risen. I punched it down and nearly toppled over myself. I couldn't even manage to do something like that?

Feeling uncomfortable, I left the dough to rise a second time. Then I warmed up some soup and served Reuven leftovers from yesterday's dinner. My hands trembled from the weight of the laden plate when I carried it to the table.

Reuven noticed. "Malia, this is ridiculous. You're really worn out. Let me drive you to Dr. Shapiro's office. We can take the kids with us and—"

"No, it's okay," I said. "But I think I'll take the car instead of walking."

I still wasn't feeling hungry, but I kept Reuven company while he ate. At 12:40, I went upstairs to get my pocketbook.

"Malia, let me drive you," Reuven said as he came out of the kitchen into the hallway. "You look so pale. You can relax and leave the driving to me."

"No, I'm fine," I said firmly. "I am perfectly capable of driving a few blocks. Don't worry about me."

Reuven looked doubtful, but he let it go. I said my good-byes quickly before he had a chance to reconsider and insist on driving me again.

Fifteen minutes later I was in Dr. Shapiro's office.

Dr. Shapiro is an extraordinary woman. She's so caring, so devoted and meticulous. I'd heard her say many times that she was only Hashem's messenger, but she was a messenger in whom I had the utmost confidence.

It felt a little strange to walk into her waiting room without my children in tow. It actually looked more like a playroom than a doctor's office. I sat down to wait my turn and almost fell asleep before I was called inside.

"Sorry to keep you waiting, Malia," Dr. Shapiro said. "Now, what's this about a blood test? What's wrong?" She looked me over carefully. "Have you been crying recently?"

"No," I said, surprised. "We've had plenty of celebrations in the family, but nothing to cry about. Why?"

"Your eyes are very puffy." She frowned. "Well, let's take your temperature, and then I'll take that blood test."

I was so weak I literally could not keep the thermometer steady. I was running a fever of 101. Dr. Shapiro took a few cultures, then gave me a quick finger prick and took a blood sample.

"This will be ready in a few minutes," she said. "I'll be right back."

When she returned, she looked worried.

"What is it?" I asked anxiously.

"The numbers are wacky." She shook her head. "I'm going to take another blood test."

She pricked my finger again and examined the results as soon as possible. From the expression on her face, I could see that the numbers were still "wacky."

"Something's not right here. I'm going to send you to the lab to have some additional blood work done." She paused for a moment, then continued carefully. "Tell me, Malia, is there any history of breast cancer in your family?"

I stared at her. "No, no, nothing like that. Why?"

She scribbled on a notepad. "I'm sorry. Just routine questioning." She tore the sheet off the notepad. "Take this to the lab. They'll get these blood tests done immediately."

I glanced down at the sheet of paper. Under the scrawled list of blood tests, Dr. Shapiro had written "STAT." Mother, who knew these things from her experience as an EMT, once told me that it means "immediately." Pronto. The urgency made my skin crawl.

Dr. Shapiro patted my arm. "Just have those blood tests done," she repeated reassuringly. "Then go home and get some rest, okay?"

"Okay. Thanks a lot. Have a good Shabbos." As I got up to leave, Dr. Shapiro held me back for a moment.

"One more thing," she said. "I think it would be a good idea to check the *mezuzos* in your apartment."

Can you imagine a doctor who tells you to check your *mezuzos*? But that is Dr. Shapiro.

I nodded numbly. "All right. I'll tell my husband when I get home."

I drove to the lab for the blood tests and then headed home, feeling utterly exhausted. Strangely enough, I wasn't nervous, only resigned. Wacky blood counts, Dr. Shapiro had said. I was probably anemic or something, like my mother suspected. As for asking me about breast cancer, she'd said it was routine questioning.

Wacky blood counts? Maybe it's mono, I thought suddenly. Uh-oh! I hope it's not mono! I can't get mono now! Reuven's in *kollel* and starting the new *zman* next week. Who will take care of my children?

I staggered into my parents' house and went upstairs. Reuven was waiting for me.

"What did she say?" he asked anxiously.

"She sent me to a lab for more tests," I told him as I sat down heavily on the edge of my bed. "She said . . ." I stopped for a moment, feeling nervous all over again. "She said that we should check our *mezuzos*."

Reuven leaned against the door, frowning. "She said that?"

I nodded.

"Okay, then." He pushed himself upright and gave me a reassuring smile. "I can still take care of that this afternoon. Why don't you lie down for a little while? I'll probably be back before you wake up."

"All right. I will." The idea of a nap suddenly sounded very appealing.

Reuven smiled at me again. "Don't worry. Everything will be fine, *im yirtzeh Hashem*. I'll see you when I get back."

Reuven left the room. I kicked off my shoes and flopped onto my bed. I was soon fast asleep, blissfully oblivious to what the next several hours would bring.

A Serious 3 *Condition*

When I awoke from my nap, I felt even worse. I was weak and dizzy, with shooting headaches that seemed to stab through my brain every few minutes. I came downstairs and found it was only a few hours before Shabbos. Mother was in the kitchen, putting the last finishing touches on the Shabbos food.

"How are you feeling, Malia?" she greeted me.

"Not very good," I admitted. I sat down at the table, propping my head with one hand. "Where's Reuven?"

"He didn't get back from the *sofer* yet. I'm sure he'll be back soon."

"Did Dr. Shapiro call?"

"No, not yet." Mother frowned. "I hope she gets your blood test results before Shabbos. I'd hate to spend the whole Shabbos wondering what's happening."

This waiting was beginning to get on everyone's nerves. It was time to change the subject. As I groped for something else to talk about, I noticed a pile of oddly shaped objects on the kitchen counter.

"What are those, Ma?" I asked. "Some kind of cake?"

Mother smiled. "Those things? Those are your *challos*, Malia."

"They're what?"

Mother picked up one of the blobs. "Your father came home for a little while and saw that the dough had risen. No one was around, so he decided to be helpful and put the *challos* in the oven himself. Then he left." She chuckled. "Nobody told him that it has to be braided first! He'll be back pretty soon. I wonder if he'll be able to guess what these things are."

The phone rang. It was two hours to Shabbos.

It was Dr. Shapiro. Mother gave me the phone, but I pushed it away.

"You take it, please," I said. "I'm not clear-minded. My head is splitting, and I feel faint. Reuven's not here. You talk to her."

Mother nodded gravely.

"Dr. Shapiro," she spoke into the phone, "Malia is not feeling well, and she'd rather you talk through me. Is that all right with you?"

"It's perfectly fine, Mrs. Greenberg," Dr. Shapiro. "I'm not surprised that Malia is feeling out of it. Her condition is very serious. She needs to be hospitalized immediately."

Of course, I didn't hear what Dr. Shapiro had said, but the look on my Mother's face told me everything.

She covered the speaker and said to me, "We have to go to the hospital. Right now."

I suppose I had been expecting this. I nodded weakly. "Just take care of it, Mother. Use your best judgment."

Mother has always been a bulwark of strength for her family, her students, her friends, everyone. This was no time to fall apart, and before my eyes, I saw her pull herself together. I saw an efficient calmness come over her, and I felt reassured. There is no one I'd rather have by my side in a crisis than my mother.

"I'm sorry, Dr. Shapiro," she spoke into the phone. "I just wanted to tell Malia what you had said. Okay. Let's deal with it. What do we do?"

"It seems your daughter has a very serious problem. She is going to need top specialists. As I said, she needs to be hospitalized right away. And there's no telling how long she'll have to stay in the hospital."

"I understand," Mother said. "We'll get some things together and leave right away."

"You must make a decision now, Mrs. Greenberg," Dr. Shapiro said in a gentle voice. "Where do you want to send Malia?"

"What are our options?" Mother asked. She looked at me and gave me a reassuring smile, suppressing the dreadful alarm growing inside her heart.

"Well, certain hospitals in Manhattan may be more advanced," Dr. Shapiro pointed out. "Of course, she wouldn't be seen by the specialists until after the weekend. On the other hand, Maimonides Hospital is right here in Boro Park. At this stage, you might prefer a hospital closer to home. You must decide right now."

"We'll go to Maimonides," Mother said quietly. "We can always transfer her later if we have to. Now, it's important that she be close to home with her family nearby all the time to give her support."

"I agree," said Dr. Shapiro. "Let's just get her into a good hospital under expert medical care. Afterwards, we'll take it from there."

"Could you make the arrangements?"

"Of course," Dr. Shapiro said. "I'll speak to Dr. Nawabi right away and get back to you. He's the head of the Hematology Oncology Department in Maimonides. In the meantime, make sure Malia rests and drinks lots of liquids."

Mother hung up the phone and turned to me.

"You heard," she said carefully. "Why don't you go sit down in the dining room? Rachel will pack your things for you."

I was in a daze. I'd never even been sick before, and now I had to go the hospital? Could this really be happening?

Numbly, I allowed Mother to guide me to one of the armchairs in the dining room. My head was spinning with bewilderment, and the stabbing headaches weren't helping. Weak and dizzy, I sank into the comfortable chair. I heard Mother whispering to Rachel in the hallway, and I heard Rachel gasp. Meanwhile, Moshe and Eli came home and were also apprised of the situation. Then Mother came back into the dining room and hovered over me. Rachel ran upstairs to pack my things.

Just then Reuven walked in. He looked from me to Mother, then back at me. It didn't take much to realize something was terribly wrong.

"Okay, Malia," he said. "Tell me."

I started to speak, but I just didn't have the strength. I signaled weakly to my mother with a limp hand to speak for me.

"Dr. Shapiro called, Reuven," she said. "It looks serious. She needs to be admitted to the hospital immediately."

"What is it?" he asked. "What did she say?"

"She didn't say," Mother replied.

"Well, what could it be?"

"I couldn't say. Let the doctors tell us."

Reuven and I could both see that she had her suspicions, but we didn't press her. We'd hear the answers soon enough straight from the doctors. Why put her on the spot? As it turned out, her guess was correct.

"Okay, did you make arrangements?" Reuven asked.

"Dr. Shapiro is making the arrangements," Mother said. "It doesn't look like this is going to be a quick thing, like a day or two. From what Dr. Shapiro said, it sounds like it could be weeks or months. We had to decide if we should go to Maimonides or one of the Manhattan hospitals. You weren't here, and Malia was out of it. She asked me to decide. I chose Maimonides."

"Good," said Reuven. "I would have done the same. Malia needs lots of visitors and company to keep up her spirits. And besides, if she goes into Maimonides, we can always change later, right?"

"Of course."

"Fine, that's that. We need to make arrangements for the children. I'll call my parents and tell them what's happening. I'm sure my mother will help. Anyway, what should we be doing for Malia right now? Compresses? Tylenol? Something?"

"Lots of liquids," Mother said. "Dr. Shapiro said to give her lots of liquids."

Reuven doesn't let the grass grow under his feet. He began bringing me glass after glass of warm cranberry juice, urging me to drink. I sipped slowly and tried to smile.

"I'll be all right," I told him with a confidence I didn't feel. "I'll go into the hospital and get whatever-it-is cleared up. By the way, what happened with the *mezuzos*?"

"One of them had to be fixed," Reuven replied. "I replaced it with a new one."

"Good," I said.

Then I began to feel faint. Mother realized what was happening and had me lie down immediately, with my feet elevated. Now I was really frightened. Something was terribly wrong.

While all this was going on, my oldest brother Gavriel and his wife Frieda stopped by to drop off the suitcase Rachel was to take back to Israel for them on Motzaei Shabbos.

"Hello!" my oldest brother called in his cheerful voice from the doorway. "Where is everybody?"

"We're in here!" Reuven called back. "Malia's going to the hospital!"

Gavriel and Frieda rushed into the dining room, where I was lying on two chairs. Reuven was holding both children in his arms.

"What's going on?" Gavriel asked.

"We don't know yet," Mother said, keeping her voice calm. "That's what we have to find out. Malia did some blood tests, and Dr. Shapiro feels she needs to be hospitalized over Shabbos. Reuven and I will go with her. We'll be leaving pretty soon."

For a long moment, there was silence as the news sank in. Then Frieda asked, "What are you going to do with the kids?"

"I'll be here," Rachel pointed out. "I can help take care of them. I don't think I'm going to be going back to Israel this Motzaei Shabbos."

"I have a better idea," Frieda said.

She disappeared into the kitchen. I heard her talking rapidly into the telephone. When she returned, she reached out and took Dov's hand.

"Come on, Dov," she said with determined cheerfulness. "How would you like to spend Shabbos with Uncle Gavriel and me? You can play with cousin Shimshi!"

Dov was delighted at the suggestion. He loved playing with my nephew Shimshi, and since Frieda and Gavriel live in Israel, he didn't often get the chance to spend time with him. Thankfully, he was still too young to realize there was something wrong with me, and he wasn't afraid to leave me.

I was so grateful to Frieda for her offer, but I couldn't help objecting. "This is your last Shabbos in America, for this trip, Frieda. This is your last Shabbos with your parents. Do you really need Dov around?"

"It will be a pleasure," Frieda said firmly, giving me a warm smile. "I just spoke to my parents, and they said it would be fine. Rachel, will you come upstairs and help me pack a bag for Dov?"

A few minutes later, Gavriel, Frieda and Dov were gone. The phone rang again, and Reuven ran to the kitchen to answer it, still holding Ari in his arms.

"What are we going to do with Ari?" I said slowly. "He's still nursing full-time!"

Mother squeezed my hand. "We'll take care of your baby for you," she soothed me. "Rachel will be here. Don't worry."

Reuven was back. The phone call had been nothing important.

"I'll go get some Isomil, or Pro-Sobee, or whatever's at the pharmacy," he volunteered.

"But Ari doesn't take a bottle," I protested. "I don't think he's had more than two or three bottles since he was born."

"He'll have to manage," Mother said. "Like the rest of us."

The phone rang again, and Reuven ran to get it. In a minute, he was back.

"That was Dr. Shapiro," he said. "They're expecting us at Maimonides. She's arranged for Dr. Nawabi and Dr. Ruben to take care of Malia." He looked at me. "We'd better get going."

There was no time for me to nurse my precious baby. Moshe gave us a package containing grape juice and *challos*. Then he wished me a *refuah sheleimah* and hurried down the block to buy formula for Ari before the pharmacy closed. Shabbos was just around the corner. There was no time to lose. I kissed Ari and hugged him tightly before I allowed Mother and Reuven to lead me out to the car. Reuven was carrying the bag Rachel had packed for me. The whole thing seemed completely unreal.

I turned back to look at the house as Reuven drove away. I wondered when I would see those warm, familiar walls again. From what Dr. Shapiro had said, it might be a long, long time. I remember thinking that my father still had no inkling of what was going on. When he would come home and find out, I would already be gone.

When we got to Maimonides Hospital, we made our way to the Emergency Room waiting area, as Dr. Shapiro had instructed us. We sat down on the uncomfortable plastic chairs, expecting the usual long wait before anything would happen.

We had only been waiting for about five minutes when I heard a familiar voice. There was my brother David! He and Tova were in Boro Park for Shabbos, staying at her parents' home, and Rachel had called to tell him what was happening. David, who would do anything for a friend or relative at any hour of the day or night, had hurried over to see what he could do.

"How long have you been waiting here?" he asked.

"Only a couple of minutes." I smiled at him, squinting through my headache. "How did you manage to get here so fast?"

"I'm very talented. Listen, is there anything I can do?"

"We don't know what's happening yet," Reuven explained. "You know how it is in hospitals. It'll probably be another two hours before we're even called in."

David glanced at his watch. Shabbos was only a few minutes away. "All right, then. I'll come back later to check on you."

"Thank you, David." Mother said. "We appreciate it. But please don't mention anything to your in-laws. There's no need to let the Rubinsteins know what's happening."

"Of course," David said. "I'll just explain things to Tova without telling anyone else. *Refuah Sheleimah*, Malia. I'll see you later."

I settled back into my chair. To my surprise, we waited only a few minutes more before the loudspeaker came to life. "Malia Panzer, Malia Panzer, please come to the main desk. Malia Panzer, Malia Panzer, please come to the main desk."

I looked at Mother and Reuven in disbelief. "Already? But it usually takes hours! Since when do you get in to see a doctor when it's actually time for your appointment?"

"We must be lucky," Reuven said.

I laughed at his gallows humor. It was so awful that it was actually funny.

As we approached the main desk, a man in a white coat greeted us.

"I'm Dr. Richard Ruben," he introduced himself. "Mrs. Panzer? Follow me, please. The two of you can come as well."

We followed him into one of the small rooms off the main Emergency Room. I sat on the padded examining table while Dr. Ruben asked me all the routine questions, including a rundown of any allergies or childhood illnesses. I kept answering "no." I'd never been sick before.

"Any children?"

"Yes. Two boys, aged two years and five months."

When Dr. Ruben heard that both deliveries had been natural childbirth, he chuckled. "If that's the case, this bone marrow test will be a breeze," he told me.

"Bone marrow test?" I repeated.

"Yes." Dr. Ruben put down my medical form and explained. "I'm going to take a sample of your bone marrow. There will be two parts to this. First, I'll aspirate some of the liquid, and then I'll perform a biopsy by chipping off a small piece of bone. We'll get the initial results in an hour. The full analysis won't be ready until Monday." He smiled kindly. "Don't worry. I'll let you know when it's going to hurt."

I'd heard about bone marrow tests before, and I knew they were supposed to be very uncomfortable. But Dr. Ruben was open and honest with me. I liked that. Hopefully, this wouldn't be too difficult.

I changed into a hospital gown and then turned so that my back was to the doctor. I could still hear his voice, calm and reassuring, telling me exactly what was going to happen.

"I'm making a pen mark," Dr. Ruben told me. I could feel a tiny circle being drawn on my back. "Now I'm going to use a needle to anesthetize the area." He paused for a moment. "You're going to feel a sharp pain now."

I gasped and cringed as the long needle went deep into my back. It was an excruciatingly sharp, burning sensation. After a few moments, the pain subsided, and I knew that the anesthesia had taken effect.

"Okay, Malia, you're doing great. Now I'm going to use a second needle to aspirate some bone marrow."

I could feel blood dripping. I twisted my head around and watched as Dr. Ruben smeared my bone marrow onto a glass slide. "Is that it?" I asked.

"Not quite." He picked up a second tool. "That was your bone marrow. Now I'm going to chip off a very small part of your pelvic bone. It won't hurt. You'll just feel a lot of pressure."

Sure enough, there wasn't really any pain. I could feel a pushing, tugging sensation, but it didn't hurt.

"You have very hard bones," Dr. Ruben noted as he chipped away at the bone. "Very dense and strong. That's why it's taking so long."

That surely is a good sign, I thought to myself. I wondered if Dr. Ruben thought that strong, healthy bones meant there was nothing wrong with me.

Finally, Dr. Ruben straightened up. My samples were safely smeared onto glass slides, and the site was cleaned and bandaged. The bone marrow test was over.

"All right, Malia. We're finished here. Try to relax. I'm going to take these samples to the lab to be analyzed."

"How long will it take?" Mother asked.

"As I said, we'll get the preliminary results from the aspirate in an hour, but we won't have an answer on the biopsy until Monday." He gave us one last reassuring smile. "We'll tell you what's happening as soon as we can." With a final wave of his hand, he rushed from the room, leaving the three of us staring at each other, wondering what was going to happen next.

Time passed slowly. I dozed on the same padded table where the bone marrow test had been taken. Reuven said *Kaballas Shabbos*, the first time ever without a *minyan*. Mother said it as well, sitting right next to me. Simply by being there, she was giving me enormous comfort.

Almost two hours had gone by since Dr. Ruben had left with my samples. Wasn't it only supposed to take an hour? Looking at Reuven and Mother, I could see they were thinking the same thing: the longer it took to get the results, the more we realized that things were more complicated than we had thought.

"We have to be strong," I said into the silence.

Reuven nodded. "Yes, Malia. I hope, I pray that everything will be all right, but we're all going to be here for each other, no matter what."

"You have our support, Malia," Mother added. "And you have our love. With Hashem's help, we are all going to pass this test with flying colors."

The tension in the room was almost visible. We were anxiously waiting, hoping, preparing ourselves for whatever might happen. Over and over, we told ourselves we would accept whatever Hashem gives us. Whatever the results, whatever the circumstances, we would face this test with love and determination.

The door opened. Dr. Ruben entered the room together with Dr. Nawabi, head of Hematology/Oncology. Dr. Nawabi closed the door behind them.

I sat up on the table. Reuven stopped pacing. Mother rose from her seat.

Dr. Nawabi faced me and said quietly, "Malia, you have something seriously wrong with your bone marrow. You will have to be hospitalized for at least a month while we try to solve your problem."

At least a month? I could hardly believe this was happening. I hadn't been a weak, sickly child. I'd never been sick at all! A month in the hospital? Didn't that happen to other people? I could feel warm tears trickling down my cheeks. What about Reuven? What about my kids? What was going to happen?

I was too exhausted and feeling too miserable to question Dr. Nawabi further. It didn't even occur to me that he hadn't given me a full diagnosis of what was wrong.

"Don't worry, Malia," Reuven said, offering me a brave smile. "We'll take care of ourselves. And of you, too."

Mother didn't say anything, but she was grateful to Dr. Nawabi for not being specific and for not frightening me more than necessary. It was enough for me to know I had something serious. For Mother, the bone marrow test and the doctors' reactions was all the proof she needed to realize the truth.

I had leukemia.

Questions and Answers

We returned to the admitting office to fill out all the necessary forms. Name, address, age. I couldn't even answer these simple questions. Reuven had to answer for me. Everything was happening at a distance, through a thick haze.

Then the office asked Dr. Nawabi for the name of my primary doctor. That was when I heard Dr. Sam Kopel's name for the first time.

When all the forms were completed, an orderly arrived with a wheelchair to escort me to my room.

"The Gellman Building, eighth floor," Dr. Nawabi told the orderly. "Room 5832."

"We'll be there soon," Reuven promised. He and Mother would walk up the eight flights of stairs, since Shabbos had already begun. There were Shabbos elevators that stopped automatically at every floor, but these were mostly for the use of the patients.

As the elevator doors closed behind me, Dr. Nawabi and Dr. Ruben remained with Mother and Reuven for a few more minutes.

"I didn't want to say so in front of Malia," Dr. Nawabi said gently, "but her bone marrow test indicates that she has leukemia."

"Leukemia!" Reuven was devastated. He'd never even considered that as a possibility. Tears streamed from his eyes. His entire world seemed to cave in. His wife had leukemia!

For Mother, Dr. Nawabi's words were less shocking. They were only a confirmation of her worst fears. She tried to stay calm and strong. "We are religious people," she told the two doctors. "We have faith in the Creator. Whatever He does is for the best."

Dr. Nawabi nodded gravely. "With Heaven's help, Malia will be cured," he assured her. "Time and time again, I've seen that when a patient is religious and has strong family support, there is a much greater chance of full recovery."

"Malia doesn't realize," Reuven whispered. "She doesn't know what's happening."

"It's better that way," Dr. Nawabi explained. "We'll give it a chance to sink in gradually. At this point, I'd rather not frighten her."

After the doctors had patiently answered several more questions, Reuven and Mother climbed the eight flights of stairs to my room. Reuven, who is such a caring husband, waited outside my room for a few minutes until he was more composed and his eyes were no longer red. He didn't want to frighten me. The truth was, though, that I probably wouldn't have noticed a five-piece band marching through my room. I was too exhausted and dazed to comprehend what was happening to me.

Before Mother and Reuven arrived, I had a few minutes to meet my new roommate. She was an older woman, about sixty years old, with thin lips, a pointy nose and smiling eyes. She was sitting up in bed when I was wheeled into the room. She wore a pink turban on her head.

"Hello," she said, smiling. She was always smiling. Even when she was feeling sick and weak, her eyes still smiled. "I'm Rose Scheiner."

"I'm Malia Panzer," I said. She seemed like a nice, friendly person.

"Why are you here?" she asked.

"There's something wrong with my bone marrow," I said vaguely, not really knowing any more.

"I've been here for a while," she said. "I have stomach cancer. They can't do much to treat it."

It was a little shocking to hear this. If we were roommates in the same hospital ward, did that mean I had an illness of similar magnitude? It was another hint that things were a lot worse than I realized, but I was too exhausted to absorb the implications.

We spoke for a few more minutes before some nurses arrived and began bustling around my bed. Then the curtains were drawn, and Rose and I couldn't talk any more.

Then Mother walked in, and Reuven a minute or two later.

"How are you doing, Malia?" Reuven asked anxiously.

"I'm okay," I said, feeling very tired. It was almost too much effort to talk. I was running a fever, I had a terrible headache, and I hadn't nursed for hours, leaving me feeling very uncomfortable. Reuven and Mother realized this and didn't try to make conversation.

The *challah* and grape juice Moshe had given us before we left the house had been left behind in the car in our rush to get to the Emergency Room. We had nothing for a Shabbos meal. After a while, two pleasant nurses came in and offered us peanut butter sandwiches and apple juice.

"The perfect Shabbos meal," Reuven joked.

In the end, a religious Jew in another room offered us some *challah,* and we managed to get some grape juice from the Bikur Cholim society. Mother and Reuven had a quiet little meal. I just watched. I didn't feel like eating or drinking anything.

Meanwhile, I was started on blood transfusions. The IV (intravenous) was stinging my wrist. Mother and Reuven watched nervously as the blood dripped slowly into my system. They told us it would take four and a half hours for all the blood to transfuse. Dr. Ruben stayed with us, offering encouragement, until 1:00 in the morning.

At 2:00, someone quietly walked into the room. I could hardly believe my eyes. It was David!

"How did you manage to get past security?" Reuven asked incredulously.

"Leave it to David," Mother laughed.

"I came to see how you're doing," David explained. "Have you heard anything new?"

"A little," Reuven said evasively. He still didn't want to say anything in front of me.

Just then, a nurse came in. "I'm sorry," she said politely but firmly. "Hospital policy does not allow male chaperons overnight with female patients."

"Not even a husband?" David asked.

"No, I'm afraid not. You'll both have to leave."

"Can my mother-in-law stay?" Reuven asked quickly. He didn't want to go against hospital rules, but he didn't want me to be left alone.

"Yes, that will be all right."

"Come with me," David said, taking Reuven by the arm. "My in-laws will put you up for the night. We're only a couple of blocks away. You'll do better with a couple of hours' sleep."

Reuven got up reluctantly. "I'll be back in the morning, Malia," he promised. "Don't worry."

"I won't," I mumbled.

Reuven and David left. Mother and I were left alone behind the curtain around my bed. Mother tried to doze on two chairs, but the blood transfusion was still taking place and making us too anxious to sleep. The constant stinging as the blood dripped through the IV on my wrist didn't help either. I also had an uncomfortable, itchy feeling, as if sticky plastic were plastered over my face, neck and hair. I guessed this was a reaction to the transfusion as well.

At dawn, I finally managed to fall asleep. When I awoke at 8:00 in the morning, Reuven was already sitting there.

"Good Shabbos, Malia," he said with a warm smile.

"Good Shabbos." I smiled back. "It's good to see you."

The curtains were drawn back. I could see Rose in her bed by the window.

"How are you feeling this morning?" she asked.

"Much better," I said, moving my arms and legs. "I guess the blood transfusions really helped." I did feel much stronger than I had in quite a while. "Maybe I'll take a walk soon."

"I wouldn't advise it," Rose said. "You're a lot weaker than you think you are. You'd better call a nurse if you want to get out of bed."

A little taken aback, I turned to Reuven. "Where's Mother?" I asked.

"She went back to Flatbush," he replied. "She wants to tell the family what's happening. She also said you were very worried about how Ari is doing with formula. She promised to come back with a report."

"Oh, I hope he ate something," I said anxiously. "Poor Ari. Imagine your mother just disappearing on you like that."

"It's all right, Malia. Rachel is there, and Eli, and Moshe, and your father. I'm sure that between the four of them, they'll manage."

"I hope so," I sighed.

We talked for a few minutes more before Reuven suggested that I might want to try getting out of bed.

"I really think you should wait," Rose called from her bed. "If you want to get up, you ought to talk to a nurse first."

Reuven and I looked at each other. "I'm feeling much better, but maybe she's right," I said finally. "But I don't want to call the nurse with the buzzer on Shabbos."

"I'll get a nurse for you," Reuven offered, standing up.

"No, it's okay. I'll just wait."

Sure enough, a nurse came in a few minutes later. "How are you feeling this morning?" she asked cheerfully.

"Much better," I answered. "I'd like to get out of bed, if I can."

"We'll let you try," the nurse replied, "but we'll be right here if you need help."

Carefully, I eased my legs out of bed and walked slowly to the bathroom. I was very pleased with myself at first, but after a few minutes, I began to feel dizzy and faint.

"Help!" I gasped. The nurse was there in a flash, and she and Reuven carried me straight back to bed.

I lay quietly in bed. Apparently, I was a lot weaker than I thought. Reuven sat on a chair on the side of the bed without saying anything, just offering moral support by being there.

"Don't feel bad," Rose consoled me. "In a few weeks, you'll be up and about and back to yourself."

Half an hour later, Dr. Ruben came into the room.

"Good morning, Malia," he said. He looked at Reuven. "Could I ask you to wait outside the room for a few minutes?"

Reuven nodded, gave me a smile and left the room, closing the door behind him.

"We have some plans for you this morning, Malia. We're going to put a central IV line into the large vein in your chest so that you won't have to get transfusions through your arm. Since we'll have to give you a lot of blood over the next few weeks, it will be a lot easier for you this way."

"You mean I won't have the IV needle in my arm anymore?" It certainly sounded wonderful to be able to have my arms free. Maybe it wouldn't sting so much either.

"That's right," Dr. Ruben said. "It'll save the veins in your arm, and we won't have to keep putting in a new needle." He paused for a moment. "We'll also have to give you a chest X-ray."

"Why?" I asked.

"Two reasons," Dr. Ruben explained. "First of all, we have to make sure that when Dr. Plantilla puts in the central line, your lungs aren't damaged. It's rare for that to happen, but we like to check just to make sure."

"I understand," I said. "And the second reason?"

"We have to check your lungs," Dr. Ruben said carefully, "because people with leukemia are very susceptible to pneumonia."

Leukemia! I don't think Dr. Ruben realized I hadn't been told yet. He just let the news drop casually. But I'd already realized that I had something very serious, and I was sort of expecting to hear something of this nature. After hearing about Rose's stomach cancer, it wasn't such a shock. I didn't cry or go into denial. I just accepted it. I didn't know that much about leukemia, but I had heard it was curable. Thank Heaven for that, at least. It could have been worse.

Dr. Ruben sat down in Reuven's chair to explain further. "The bone marrow is the place where your blood cells are manufactured. When a person has leukemia, it means something has gone wrong with the blood-making factory in his or her bone marrow. To put it very simply, there are three main components to your blood: red blood cells, white blood cells and platelets. The red blood cells carry oxygen to the brain, the white blood cells fight infections, and the platelets help your blood clot when you bleed." He paused. "All clear so far?"

"Yes," I said. I was grateful that he was taking the time to explain this to me.

"All right," he continued. "Now, another word for white blood cells is leukocytes. The problem starts when immature leukocytes, for some unknown reason, multiply abnormally, much faster than usual. These immature leukocytes crowd out the healthy ones, and since they're incapable of doing the right job, the person gets leukemia. Right now, your bone marrow is filled with thousands and thousands of these immature white blood cells. They've crowded out all the healthy cells, as well as the red blood cells and platelets."

"I understand," I said, trying to picture what was happening inside my body. "Is that why I've been having headaches and feeling so weak?"

"The two are tied together," Dr. Ruben said. "You don't have enough red blood cells to carry oxygen to your brain, so you feel faint."

"I did feel very dizzy when I got out of bed before," I admitted.

"Exactly. Now another thing. With your white blood count so low, you're very susceptible to infection. That's why we'll have to check you for pneumonia, and anyone who's sick is going to have to stay away from you. We'll have to isolate you in a private room pretty soon."

Isolation? I decided to save my questions until he was finished.

"And that's not the end of it. Without enough platelets, bleeding can be dangerous. Your blood can't clot properly, so there's a danger of hemorrhaging." He gave me a reassuring smile. "The fact that you gave birth without trouble only five months ago is a good sign, Malia. If your leukemia had already developed by then, you could have hemorrhaged badly. That means that we've caught it pretty early, and there's a better chance of recovery."

Thank Heaven, I thought gratefully. Hashem has given me the best possible chance of being cured. And, the doctors said, since I'd been nursing full-time, I would avoid certain other complications as well.

"You have other things going for you, too," Dr. Ruben added. "You're young—only twenty-two—and you're in good physical shape." He smiled. "You're also religious. Believe me, that's a big plus when it comes to dealing with an illness like this."

It's a big plus when it comes to anything, I thought. But I let the remark pass without comment.

"So what are we going to do about it?" I asked.

"There are two steps," Dr. Ruben told me. "First comes the induction. We have to put you into remission. That means killing the leukemic cells and getting the numbers of your blood count up to safe levels. Once we've accomplished that, we'll see about curing you. I should explain that leukemia itself isn't painful, but the treatment can be very uncomfortable. We have to use very powerful medications to destroy the immature leukocytes, and there can be some pretty bad side reactions."

"*Im yirtzeh Hashem*, it'll all work out," I said sincerely. "Hashem is watching over me. We're going to fight and beat the leukemia!"

"That's the spirit." Dr. Ruben smiled again as he stood up. "Dr. Plantilla will be coming in pretty soon. You're scheduled for another blood transfusion this afternoon, so we want to get your central port fixed up. I'll be back later to talk to you again and answer any questions you might have."

I watched him leave the room, grateful for having a sincere, honest doctor who took the time to make things clear to me.

Reuven came back into the room. He looked at me with a question in his eyes.

"He told me," I said quietly. "I know it's leukemia."

Reuven sat down slowly, watching my face. After a moment, he smiled. He could see I was really okay, that I was taking it well.

"We'll get through this, Malia," he said softly.

"I know," I said. "We'll get through this together."

Family Decisions

It was 7:30 in the morning when Mother left the hospital to go back to Flatbush. She was still wearing her sneakers from Erev Shabbos, so the walk wasn't too difficult. Along the way, she met many people she knew. They all greeted her with broad smiles, assuming she was on her way to some kind of a joyous occasion. Mother merely smiled at them and returned their greetings without giving them any indication of the turmoil in her heart.

Mother went straight to the *shul* that Father always attended. She had someone call him out into the hall, and right there, she told him exactly what was happening.

"How definite is it that Malia has leukemia?" he asked softly.

"They won't have the final answer until Monday," Mother answered, "but the doctors don't seem to question it."

The blood drained from his face, but there was nothing he could do to help except go back into *shul* to pour out his heart to Hashem. What greater help could he give?

Mother went home. She reassured Rachel that I was in good hands and that tests were being taken. For her part, Rachel told Mother that they hadn't had an easy time with Ari. He wasn't interested in Isomil or Pro-Sobee; he wanted his mommy! Despite coaxing, singing, and all kinds of distractions from his aunt, uncles and grandfather, Ari kept crying and refusing to take the bottle. Finally, Ari drank a few ounces, apparently his hunger had gotten the best of him. By the time Mother came home, he was already reconciled to the idea of drinking formula.

"Tell me," Rachel said, "how is Malia? What's happening? Is it mono? Do they know what's wrong with her?"

"I told you," said Mother. "They're taking tests. We should know more in a few days." Mother didn't want to speak about cancer or leukemia to anyone other than Father until it was absolutely necessary.

Rachel, though, had done more guessing than Mother had realized. Since Mother is a volunteer EMT and a CPR instructor, we have lots of medical literature in the house, some of it written on a level designed for younger readers. All of us had read the books at one time or another. Just as Mother had realized the implications before Reuven, Rachel was now apprehensive about the possibilities.

Rachel hugged Ari tightly. "Does Malia have the L word?" she asked quietly.

Mother has never lied to us. She couldn't lie to Rachel now. "It's possible," she said.

Rachel was silent for a long time. She finally said, "Don't they cure it with bone marrow transplants?"

"I think so," Mother said. She wasn't entirely sure. Transplanting healthy marrow from a matching type into the patient's system can cure some kinds of leukemia, but did that apply in my case?

"I'm going to stay in America, Mother," Rachel said. "You need me here. I'll stay as long as I have to. I know I can help you."

Mother hesitated. Rachel would certainly be a great help to her, but was it right to deprive her of her last weeks in seminary? Rachel was also a big worrier. Would it be better for her to be here, agonizing over every little thing, or to be in Israel, wondering and worrying about what was happening?

Rachel's initial question also showed that she was thinking of a bone marrow transplant. It was true that the best chance of a match was with a sibling. But how could they know if Rachel was a match for my bone marrow? How does one get tested to find out? Was Rachel too young to donate bone marrow? Mother had no way of knowing if a bone marrow transplant was even something to consider.

"If you think it would be better for me to go, Mother, I will," Rachel added quickly. "I'll do whatever you decide. But I want you to know that I'm willing to stay if I have to."

"I don't know," Mother said at last. "I'm going back to the hospital this afternoon and talk to the doctors. Maybe they can help us decide." There wasn't much time. Rachel was scheduled to go back to Israel that very night.

Mother walked back to Maimonides Hospital early that afternoon. I was glad to see her. Dr. Plantilla had already inserted the central line into my chest and sent me for my chest X-ray to make sure my lungs were clear of pneumonia and that the central line hadn't caused any damage. *Baruch Hashem*, everything had come out clear. When Mother got back, I had already begun my second blood transfusion, this time through the central line. It was much more comfortable than an IV through the arm.

"Good Shabbos, Malia. How are you feeling?"

"Tired," I answered with a smile, "but okay."

"Is the blood transfusion giving you trouble?" she asked as she sat down in the chair next to Reuven's.

"No," I assured her. "I told Dr. Plantilla about the stinging and the itchy feeling, and he told me that they'll premedicate me from now on so I won't feel it. They gave me Tylenol and Benedryl to avoid any reactions." I lifted my free arms with a smile. "And no more needles!"

"That's good." Mother settled back into her chair.

"How's Ari doing? Did he take the formula?" I asked anxiously.

"If I'm going to have to be here for at least a month, I don't know what's going to happen to the kids!"

"He took the formula," Mother told me. "It's all right. And we'll figure out what to do with the kids. Don't worry about that."

"Mother," I said then, "I think I should tell you . . . I know."

Mother looked at Reuven, who nodded his head. "Dr. Ruben told Malia this morning," he told her.

Mother was quiet for a moment. "Did anyone say anything about starting treatment?" she finally asked.

I shook my head. "I haven't met all the doctors yet," I explained. "Only Dr. Ruben and Dr. Nawabi. Dr. Ruben talked to me this morning, but he mostly explained what leukemia really is. He did say I have to go into remission before I can be cured."

While we were still talking, Dr. Ruben came in again. Mother, who was still worried about what to do with Rachel, asked him several questions.

"My daughter is supposed to leave for Israel tonight. Should I have her stay? Does she need to be tested for a match to Malia's bone marrow?"

"It's a possibility, of course," Dr. Ruben replied. "If Malia is diagnosed as having acute myogenous leukemia, or AML, then she will probably need a bone marrow transplant to be cured. Most people with leukemia do have AML. But as for your daughter staying home instead of going to Israel—" He shook his head. "I don't think that's necessary. How long will she be away?"

"Six weeks," Mother said. "She's finishing her year in seminary."

"Then let her finish the year. We can't even think about finding a match for Malia's bone marrow until she's in remission. Then the H.L.A. testing, which is a simple blood test, can be performed. The testing is done in Manhattan at the Greater Blood Bank, but if necessary, your daughter can be tested in Israel. It will probably be better for her to finish her school year. Even if worse comes to worst, she or her bone marrow could be flown in if necessary."

Mother nodded slowly, but she still had questions. "She's also engaged. She's getting married on September eighth. Should we change the wedding date? Make it earlier, or later?"

Dr. Ruben chuckled. "No, don't change the wedding date. G-d willing, Malia will be there, dancing away!"

Soon after, Mother walked back to Flatbush again to tell Rachel that she was leaving that night after all. The two-mile walk was beginning to seem almost routine! Rachel, alone in the house with Ari, was surprised and delighted to see her.

"Father and the boys went to *shul* for *Minchah*," she said. "Mother, what's happening?"

"You're going back tonight," Mother told her with an encouraging smile. "The doctors might not even start testing for a match before you come back, and if they do, it'll be easy for you to get tested in Jerusalem."

"Are you sure?" Rachel asked uncertainly. "Maybe it would be better for me to stay."

"Yes, we're sure. Go to Israel and pray for Malia at all the holy places. What better help could you give her?"

Rachel still wasn't convinced, but when Father came home, he helped Mother persuade her that it was best for all concerned if she went back to complete her seminary year.

That evening, during *shalosh seudos,* Rachel and Mother harmonized together for the first time in almost a year. *"Gam ki eilech b'gei tzalmaves, lo ira ra, ki Atah imadi . . .* Even if I should walk in the valley of deathly shadows, I will not be afraid, for You are with me." They were moved, inspired and encouraged. Hashem is with us. We will not be afraid.

That night, Mother and Father drove Rachel to the airport for her flight back to Israel. She desperately wanted to see me before she left, but Shabbos ended so late that there was no time. Levi Goldstein and his parents also came to the airport to see her off. By now, they had heard I was hospitalized. They showed great concern and asked for details, wanting to know what they could do to help.

Mother and Father didn't elaborate, merely saying that the official test results wouldn't be available until Monday.

My grandparents, who had heard that I was hospitalized, came to visit me after Shabbos in the hospital. When they arrived, Rose was fast asleep in the other bed. I saw my grandfather staring at her with disbelief.

"What's wrong?" I finally asked in a quiet voice.

He hesitated, then leaned forward and whispered in Yiddish, "Your roommate is a man?"

I nearly burst out laughing. Rose's turban had slipped off her head, revealing a head made bald by chemotherapy. Her pleasant features did seem somewhat masculine. It was an understandable mistake. The funniest thing was that Rose spoke Yiddish perfectly and would have understood everything my grandfather said had she been awake.

Right after Shabbos, Reuven called his parents in Monsey, but he didn't tell them exactly what was really wrong with me; they only knew I was extremely anemic and had been hospitalized for blood transfusions. When he told them I would be hospitalized for at least a month, his mother immediately said, "Bring Dov and Ari to us. We'll take care of them until Malia is better."

Reuven was grateful to know that he could leave his sons in his parents' loving care. So that night, while Mother, Father and Rachel went to the airport, David drove Reuven, Moshe and my children to Monsey. My in-laws welcomed their grandchildren with open arms, relieving Reuven of one of our biggest worries. Our children would be okay. Now we could concentrate on getting me better.

Reuven told Dov that he would be staying with Bubbi and Zeidi for a while. "Mommy has a boo-boo," he explained. "When Mommy's boo-boo gets better, we'll bring you back home. Now, you'll have a good time playing with Bubbi and Zeidi!"

"Okay," Dov said cheerfully. My mature little man!

Once Dov and Ari were settled, Reuven, David, and Moshe went to see the Skverer Rebbe. The Rebbe is related to our family, and Reuven has a close personal relationship with him. Reuven, who had put up a brave front for me all Shabbos, desperately wanted to receive a blessing and clear-headed guidance.

The Rebbe gave Reuven a full half-hour of his time. He was both calming and reassuring. "You have nothing to worry about," the Rebbe told Reuven. "I personally know many people who had leukemia in the past; Most are fine now and completely back to themselves. Among all cancers, leukemia has a high rate of cure." He also approved of Dr. Shapiro's suggestion to check our *mezuzos.* "Your wife will get better," the Rebbe repeated.

Reuven was a different person when he left the Rebbe. He had received hope and encouragement for the future. With Hashem's help, we were going to beat this leukemia and return to a life of health and happiness.

The Isolation Room

News spreads quickly in the religious community. By Sunday afternoon, it seemed that half my acquaintances knew I was in the hospital. We decided not to make any mention of leukemia yet; instead, we just told everyone I was very anemic and needed blood transfusions. It was the truth, if not the whole truth.

Early Sunday afternoon, Reuven came to visit me, bringing Gavriel and David along. Mother was there, too; Father had dropped her at Maimonides on the way home from the airport the night before.

"Hi, Malia," Reuven said. He seemed much more relaxed than he had been on Shabbos. We had the Skverer Rebbe to thank for that.

"Hi." I grinned back at him. "Hey, I've got a good story for you."

"What do you mean?" Reuven asked curiously.

I settled back against the pillow. "Well, they came to take my blood last night… one of the technicians, I mean. He was Russian, and his accent is pretty heavy. Anyway, he asked me why I was here, and I told him I had leukemia." I stopped to exchange amused looks with Ma.

"Go on," Reuven urged me.

"So he looks at me for a second and then asks me, 'Are you cute or chronic?' I got really insulted. How can this guy come in here and ask me whether I'm cute or old?" I laughed. "At least, that's what I thought he was saying! Mother figured it out, though. He wanted to know whether I had acute or chronic leukemia."

"Well, I'm glad you figured it out. I wouldn't want you to be mad at the hospital staff." Reuven chuckled, although it doesn't seem so funny now that I think about it. I guess he was just being nice.

Gavriel stayed in the corner of the room, as far away from me as possible. He had a cold, and we had been warned that I had very little immunity. With such a low white blood count, I was prone to infection.

"Thanks again for taking Dov on Shabbos, Gavriel," I said gratefully. "It really took a load off my mind."

"It was our pleasure," he replied. "I'm sorry you needed the help, but we were glad to give it."

"When are you going back to Israel?" I asked.

Gavriel and David exchanged glances. "We're supposed to go back before Shabbos," Gavriel said evasively. "We'll see."

"Because of me, you mean?" I asked.

"Yes," Gavriel admitted. "I might be needed for a match."

"But Dr. Ruben said Rachel could go to Israel and get tested there," I protested. "Can't you do the same?"

"I suppose I could. I wasn't aware of that."

"We're going right after Shabbos," David added. "I suppose that will give me enough time to get tested before I go. Mother said it's just a simple blood test. Maybe Gavriel can do the same."

"Have you heard anything new?" Reuven asked me.

"I don't think I'm going to be in this room much longer," I told him. "They said something about isolation."

"What does that mean?" David asked.

Mother had been sitting quietly on a chair next to my bed. Now she joined the conversation. "From what the doctors said, Malia's white blood count is so low that she can, Heaven forbid, catch just about anything. I think they're planning to put Malia in a private room where she can't be exposed to germs."

Mother turned out to be right. Later that afternoon, soon after Eli had come to visit me on his way home from school, a nurse came by and told me to pack my things. "You're being moved to K-5," she told me.

Eli and I had been playing Skip-Bo together, but we stopped and Eli willingly helped me pack. Then he and Reuven carried all my things down to Room 6519 on the fifth floor in the Kronish Building, my home for the next several weeks.

When I'd heard the word isolation, I'd assumed it meant being in a private room, away from other contagious patients. It turned out to be a lot more than that. Room 6519 had a single bed in the center of the room, with a private bathroom only a few feet away. Not only was I not allowed to have a roommate, I was also not really allowed visitors. The door was always closed. No one could come into the room, whether doctors, nurses or visitors, without scrubbing up and wearing a mask so as not to expose me to germs. I wasn't even allowed to open the little window overlooking the courtyard between the hospital buildings, since I might catch germs from the air outside!

I'd heard comments that K-5 was the oldest, darkest, dingiest part of the hospital, but Dr. Ruben had been quite pleased that he'd managed to get me a room on that floor. "K-5 has exceptional nurses," he told me. "It's not so easy to get an isolated room there. I know they'll take good care of you there."

Mother took Eli home while Reuven helped me settle into the room. I was a little uncertain about my new surroundings; the off-white walls were bare and cheerless, and I wasn't sure I liked the open window in the door. Apparently, the window enabled nurses to check on me without having to enter the room, saving them the trouble of constantly scrubbing up in order to come inside. I supposed it made sense, but it meant there would be no such thing as privacy during my entire stay.

Reuven noticed how I looked at the bare walls. "We'll decorate it," he promised me. "Don't worry."

He was right. Over the course of my hospital stay, my walls became so colorful that many people would stop by and look into the window—not to visit me, but to stare at the decorations! We hung up a large studio photo of Dov. My dear in-laws, knowing I would also want a picture of Ari, took my five-month-old to have a professional picture taken. We hung it right next to Dov's. It meant so much to me to have those photographs of my precious children.

We taped all the dozens and dozens of get-well cards to the wall, as well as the scribbled notes of people who came to say hello and didn't want to disturb me when I was asleep. I had balloons, banners and posters. One particular favorite was a big, fat, blue balloon with a happy face and hands and feet. When my cousin Miriam gave it to me, I laughed and dubbed it Look-a-me-uh, a bad pun for the disease I was battling. Father, however, wasn't so sure he liked that name very much.

Looking at my balloons, I felt myself suddenly transported in my thoughts back to an earlier, more innocent time. Once again, I was a carefree schoolgirl in Bais Yaakov with no greater worries than my next Chumash test.

Everyone knew I was a dancer. Arms raised above my head and feet flickering on the ground, I felt like a bird in flight. I loved it, and I was also quite good at it. When I was in the tenth grade, the school put on a lavish song-and-dance production for the community, and I was given an important dancing role. I worked very hard rehearsing for that performance. Just about everyone would be in the audience watching me — my mother, my grandmother, my sister, my aunts and cousins and all my friends. I really felt the pressure.

I was so nervous on the night of the performance that I could not even eat anything. All I could manage was a few sips of water, barely enough to wet my dry lips. As I walked onto the stage, I squeezed my hands shut to keep them from shaking, but there was nothing I could do about the loud pounding of my heart, which must have been audible all the way to the back row.

Then the performance began, and everything was transformed. I became one with the sweet melodies and the rhythm of the dance movements, and my spirit soared. I could no longer hear my heart pounding, nor did I feel my hands shaking. I was all fluid motion, floating on a cloud of music.

The performance lasted nearly two hours. To me it seemed like minutes. The final curtain fell to thunderous applause, and we all took our bows. From the corner of my eye, I sought out my family. They were all standing and cheering, and my heart leaped with exquisite joy. It was a perfect moment, one of the best in my life.

Running off the stage, we were immediately swamped by friends and family. Two close friends hugged me, screaming, "Malia, you were just wonderful!"

I felt a tug from behind, and there was another of my closest friends. She hugged me. Then she shoved something into my hand and said, "Here, Malia, these are for you."

I looked down at my hand and saw a few brightly colored ribbons. For a moment, I was puzzled, but then I looked up and saw the balloons and the words written on them: "Congratulations!" There were four balloons — yellow, red, pink and green — and they were so pretty. I watched them floating high above the crowd, and I recognized the feeling. On that perfect night, I too soared high. Just me and my balloons.

My mind jumped forward two years, and I imagined myself back in school again, this time in twelfth grade, an important senior. I was sitting in the classroom together with all the other girls in my class, quiet, subdued, edgy with anticipation. The door opened, and the assistant principal came in.

"Girls," she said, "the results are in. We have the answers you've been waiting for these last two weeks."

We all stirred in our seats, and held our breaths.

"First, class president," she said. "The vote is over, and the winner is . . . Malia Greenberg!"

Pandemonium broke loose. I don't remember if I screamed or laughed or simply froze there stock-still. An instant later, I was surrounded by delirious friends hugging me and shouting their congratulations.

"Here, Malia," I heard one of them say, "these are for you."

I felt the ribbons in my hand, and I knew the balloons were there even before I saw them.

"But how did you know I was going to win?" I asked. "What if I had lost? What would you have done with the balloons?"

"Oh, come on, Malia," one friend told me, "you were a shoo-in. You were the best candidate, so of course, we knew you would win."

"That's not so!" I said, "Come on, I could just as easily have lost. Then you would have been stuck with the balloons."

"No, Malia," she said. "We wouldn't have been stuck with them. We would have given them to you because we love you, win or lose."

I hugged my friend. I was happy as a lark.

The scene in my mind shifted again. I was eighteen years old. It was towards the end of my seminary year, one of the happiest and most memorable days of my life. I was getting engaged to Reuven Panzer! The house was overflowing with people, friends, family, new in-laws, strangers smiling widely at me and saying things I couldn't really hear. And then a group of my camp friends came bursting through the door carrying what else? A cluster of gaily colored balloons. I laughed. How did they know that I loved balloons?

A few minutes later, some of my high school friends arrived, and they too brought me balloons. They had not forgotten. But then the strangest thing happened. My new sister-in-law brought me the largest, pudgiest, most colorful, most adorable bunch of balloons I had ever seen! How had they discovered my passion for balloons? To this day I still don't know, because in the excitement of the engagement I forgot to ask them.

Balloons had always held wonderful associations for me. They had marked the most joyous moments of my life, crinkly symbols of my soaring spirit. And now, as I sat in the drab solitude of the isolation room and looked at my colorful balloons, I wondered what they were doing there. Perhaps I should send them away with Reuven and only take them out after I recovered. I felt a dark cloud of despair pass over me, and I quickly shook my head to dispel it.

No, I decided, I would keep the balloons with me. They would be my symbols of joy right here in isolation, reminding me that I should be thankful for every day that I awoke in the morning, and for the great outpouring of love and friendship that the balloons represented. They would remind me that it is important to find joy even in adversity. Especially in adversity.

That first night, Reuven unpacked my things into the drawers of the little table by my bedside and into the closet. By the time he finished, it was quite late.

"Why don't you go back to Flatbush and get some sleep?" I suggested.

Reuven yawned. "Maybe you're right. I'll just rest here for a few minutes, and then I'll go."

Reuven sat down on the recliner near my bed. "Do you think you'll be all right, all alone like this?" he asked.

"I think so," I replied. "Maybe it will be a little lonely without a roommate, but it's okay so far."

We talked for a few minutes more, then Reuven leaned back and closed his eyes. After a little while, I realized that he was sound asleep. He was so exhausted from the strain of the last few days and the constant running around that he'd simply dropped off.

I smiled to myself and settled down for the night. It looked like I was going to have a roommate after all.

Blood Donations

7

Monday afternoon, I met the doctor in charge of my case for the first time. His name is Dr. Sam Kopel, and he is one of the brilliant stars of the Hematology/Oncology team. The first time this tall, stately man walked into my room I was immediately struck by the warmth and reassurance he radiated. His cheerful smile and his constant, absent-minded whistling set my mind at ease. This was no cold, distant doctor. I could talk to this man, and he would listen with caring and devotion. Experience proved my first impression right. Dr. Kopel was never anything less than wonderful. Mother considered him a messenger from Heaven. She got no argument from me.

On that first Monday, Dr. Kopel gave me a thorough physical checkup, then he patiently explained exactly what the leukemia was doing to my body. I had already heard the basics from Dr. Ruben, but I listened attentively to every word he said. This was my life we were talking about!

"During your stay here, Malia," he told me, "you are going to need between thirty and fifty pints of blood."

I was taken aback. I'd had six pints so far in three transfusions, and I'd vaguely expected that I would need more. But fifty?

"Why so many?" I asked.

"We're going to put you through a round of chemotherapy," Dr. Kopel said. "Chemo is a series of chemicals and medications given intravenously to destroy the immature, leukemic leukocytes. Unfortunately, these medications are so powerful they not only destroy the bad cells but the good cells in your bone marrow as well. All your numbers will go down to dangerously low levels: your red blood count, your platelets, your white blood count. We'll be giving you transfusions of blood and platelets to take care of that problem."

"Do you give transfusions for the white blood count, too?" I asked. "Maybe, if I had transfusions of white blood cells, I wouldn't have to stay in isolation for too long."

Dr. Kopel shook his head. "That's a good question, but I'm afraid that's not possible. We have to wait for the white blood count to go up by itself. That's why you're here in an isolated room where you can't get infected." He smiled. "Who knows? Maybe in a few years they'll figure out some way to give transfusions of white blood cells, too. But by then you'll be healthy and well, and all this will be only a memory."

I sat quietly for a moment, thinking of what Dr. Kopel had just said. New medical techniques were being discovered all the time. I felt enormously grateful to Hashem that I had contracted leukemia in 1993, and not twenty years earlier when leukemia was an invincible killer. Thank Heaven, I would not be an experiment, but a patient with a high expectation for recovery.

"But in the meantime, we only have the technology of today," Dr. Kopel was saying. "So we'll be taking periodical blood tests to find out how you're doing and what levels your blood counts have reached."

"How does that work?" Mother asked.

"It's really quite simple," Dr. Kopel said. "There's a lab right here on this floor with a special machine that counts the number of cells per sample."

Mother nodded her understanding.

"Tomorrow we'll take a mygomugascan," Dr. Kopel told me. "We have to make sure your heart can handle the strain before we begin the chemo. The day after that, G-d willing, we'll begin the chemo and put you on the road to recovery!"

After Dr. Kopel left, Reuven came, and the three of us discussed the situation.

"You know, I'm all for discretion and staying out of the public eye," Reuven declared, "but I think it's time to go public. I want to let people know what's going on. We need people to give blood and to help in many different ways. And perhaps most important, we need their prayers. We're going to fight and beat this thing, but we need all the help we can get! What do you say, Malia?"

This was my Reuven! Devout, resourceful, optimistic. "Great," I said.

I turned to Mother. "What do you think?"

"You're right," she said. "A blood drive is no simple thing. I'm sure your father will agree."

The following morning, at 9:00, Mother, Father and Reuven began making telephone calls. Within half an hour, the blood bank was crowded with people who had come to donate blood for me. Dr. Katz, the principal of Mother's school, sent the eligible seniors in shifts. My aunt's brothers-in-law and sisters-in-law in Lakewood drove in to the blood bank in Manhattan. My parents' friends, my friends, Reuven's friends, their siblings and older children, came to donate blood for me. My father's former *rosh yeshivah* had his family call every available student to urge him to donate blood. The outpouring of *chesed* was unbelievable!

By the end of the day, forty-seven people had come to the blood bank. By the following afternoon, the number had passed seventy-five. It's impossible to know the exact number of those who volunteered to give blood, since a number of people were turned away. The blood bank does not accept blood from anyone underweight, underage, anemic or with a history of hepatitis.

Mother was particularly moved by the twelfth-graders that came from Shulamith High School. Dr. Katz had sent these seventeen-year-old girls, who were all extremely eager to perform this *mitzvah*.

"Just two weeks ago, before Pesach, we were discussing the Tay-Sachs test in school," Mother told me. "All the girls were reluctant to be tested, mostly because of the pain. Now these same girls, who swooned at the thought of having a small vial of blood drawn out of their arms, are lining up to donate an entire pint!"

Esther, a friend of one of Mother's friends, was in charge of the blood and platelets department. She approached Mother and asked if there was anything she could do to help. Mother rather hesitantly asked if she would be able to organize the donations of blood and platelets over the course of my treatments.

Esther was unbelievable! She arranged all appointments, both at Maimonides for blood donations and at the Greater Blood Bank in Manhattan for platelets, where appointments were allotted with only a fifteen-minute margin of error. After each appointment was made, Esther called the donor with exact instructions. "Bring your social security number and two forms of identification. Don't take aspirin during the seventy-two hour period before you give blood, and no alcohol for forty-eight hours beforehand. Increase your fluids the day you come. Eat foods rich in calcium." Her attention to every little detail was incredible.

The nurses at the blood bank sent a message, saying that they wanted to meet this Malia Panzer. They'd never seen anything like it! Dr. Kopel told us the blood donations had broken a record, and Maimonides Hospital was actually making a profit from me.

"Really?" Reuven remarked. "Great! Let's see if they'll take it off our bill!"

It was nice to see Reuven cracking jokes, but I knew he wasn't having an easy time of it. Because of Maimonides' policy against husbands staying overnight in a patient's room, Reuven couldn't stay with me all the time. Instead, we asked Mother to stay with me, and she, being a real trooper, moved into the hospital with me for the duration. So as it turned out, Mother was with me all the time and in touch with everything happening, while Reuven spent his days running back and forth between the hospital and Monsey, where Dov and Ari were under the loving care of his parents. He was in and out of the hospital, visiting every chance he got, but very often, he wasn't there when the doctors came around. He must have felt left out of things.

On top of that, we decided it would be wisest to let our apartment go for the time being and move our things into my parents' house. There was no knowing how long I would be in the hospital and even afterwards, even in the best-case scenario, I would need a long time to recuperate under constant care. It would be a while before I could go back to being an active homemaker and mother. So in addition to everything else, Reuven had to take care of the move all by himself. He also tried to sit down and learn whenever possible. And all this with a smile, not only on the outside but on the inside as well! He is truly an amazing person.

Mother and I have always been particularly close—I'm her oldest daughter—and it seemed natural to both of us that she simply moved into the hospital with me and spent every available moment by my side. I know it could have become a thorny situation, but Reuven has such a good relationship with my parents that it presented no problem at all. It meant so much to me that Reuven felt equally comfortable with the prospect, and that he was glad Mother would be there to help me through the difficult times ahead.

That same day, I had the mygomugascan test. I went down to Radiology, where I was escorted into a room with a computer table, a bizarre-looking machine with something that looked like a blue bicycle wheel and a narrow black bench draped with a white sheet. My aunt Shani came from Lakewood to give me moral support.

"Lie down, please," the radiologist instructed.

"On that?" I pointed incredulously at the bench. It was so narrow that it would take a major balancing act to avoid falling off. How did they possibly run this test on someone who was heavy, or even a few pounds overweight?

"Wonder what they do for football players?" Aunt Shani said, as if reading my thoughts.

I laughed.

"Just lie down, please," the radiologist repeated patiently.

Gingerly, I lay down on the narrow bench.

"Don't sneeze," Shani warned me.

I laughed again and nearly fell off. The radiologist was beginning to look irritated.

A nurse came in and hung a bright blue bag on my IV pole.

"What's that for?" Shani asked.

"We're injecting a blue dye into Malia's blood," the nurse explained. "Then the machine will pick up the blue dye and enable the doctor to see exactly what kind of shape her heart is in."

"Don't feel blue, Malia," Shani said in mock sympathy. "It won't last too long."

The test began. The radiologist carefully guided a large, thick cylinder over my body so that only my eyes and feet were showing.

It didn't hurt. Like X-rays, there was no real sensation of the pictures being taken. The only problem was that I was supposed to lie still so that the pictures would come out clear, and Shani kept making jokes. I was laughing so hard that the radiologist found it impossible to get clean, well-defined images.

Finally, he lost his patience. "Look, lady," he said to Shani. "Do me a favor and wait outside, okay? I'm never going to finish while you're here!"

Grinning sheepishly, Shani gave me a cheerful wave of her hand and left the room. I made an effort to remain still, even though I still felt like giggling at her outrageous wisecracks.

Finally, the radiologist straightened up with a look of relief. "We're all finished," he announced.

The cylinder was lifted away. I sat up on the narrow bench.

"Can I see?" I asked.

"Sure thing." He waved a hand at the computer screens on the desk. I leaned over for a closer look. There were beautiful patterns of color generated on the screens, but I had no idea what they were supposed to be.

"Is that my heart?" I asked doubtfully.

The radiologist nodded, tracing several lines with his finger. "See?" he said. "Everything is strong and healthy."

"*Baruch Hashem*," I said. I didn't see how the lines he pointed out were any different from the rest of the image, but I took his word for it.

I was taken back to my isolated room in K-5. Mother was still there, wearing her mask and gloves. It already seemed normal to see only half of Mother's face, with her warm, loving smile hidden from sight.

"Father's coming tomorrow," she said. "He wants to bring a special *mezuzah* for the door."

I nodded. Although Maimonides did have *mezuzos,* we wanted to be extra careful with this *mitzvah*, particularly since one of the *mezuzos* in our apartment had been flawed. "What's new with the family?" I asked.

Mother settled back in her chair. "We heard from Rachel," she began. "She's settled nicely back into seminary. She's pretty worried about you, though. Maybe we can arrange for you to call her later."

"I'd like that," I said. "What about the boys?"

"Moshe is back in Philly. As for Eli, he asked me for permission to spend these coming weeks, while you're in the hospital and I'm here with you, with the Chopps."

"By Lèlè?"

"Yes. He was very mature about it. He explained that he wanted to be surrounded by kids and happiness, instead of staying in a quiet house and worrying about you and the whole situation. He promised to check in with Father every day to find out what's happening and to let us know that he's doing okay."

"It sounds like a good idea to me," I agreed. At the same time, I felt a pang at the realization of how much my illness was disrupting our family. We no longer had our apartment. Mother was spending her nights and every spare moment of her days here in the hospital. Eli was moving out of the house for the duration. It wasn't simple to submit to the turmoil I'd caused, but our family's warm closeness made it easier to accept. I knew that all these hardship were being accepted willingly, and with love.

Reuven came by a little later. "I just spoke to your father," he told me. "Malia, whenever you have a chance, and you're feeling up to it, try and call Zeidi and Bubbi Greenberg in Jerusalem. They're very worried about you."

"Has anyone told them exactly what's wrong?" I asked.

Reuven grinned ruefully. "Well, that's really the problem. When Rachel went to visit them, they asked her what was wrong. She told them it was leukemia, and they wanted to know more about it, so . . ." He shrugged helplessly. "They looked it up in their 1935 almanac!"

"Oh, no!" I exclaimed.

Mother, too, looked distressed at the thought of how her in-laws must be worrying about me. Only twenty years ago, leukemia had been considered almost inevitably fatal. You can imagine how it must have been described in an almanac printed close to sixty years ago!

"So, like I said, they're pretty worried. I know it's a lot to ask, but as soon as you're feeling strong enough to call, try. Okay?"

"No problem," I assured Reuven. "I'll call them this afternoon."

We talked a little longer, until the shadows slanting through my window told us that it was late afternoon.

Mother looked at her watch and cleared her throat. "Malia."

"Yes, Mother?"

"How are you feeling? A little better?"

I smiled. "You want to call Eretz Yisrael?"

"Only if you're up to it."

"You're worried about Zeidi and Bubbi, aren't you?"

Mother nodded. "Yes, I am. They'll feel so much better if they hear your voice. They must be climbing the walls in Jerusalem, being so far away at such a time. It wouldn't surprise me if they stepped off the next plane."

"Well, I sure hope they don't do that," said Reuven. "Malia, I think you should talk to them and calm them down."

"Yes, I think so, too," I said. "I'm all right — I can handle a telephone call to Jerusalem."

I saw Mother hesitate, as if she were about to say something but then thought better of it. I knew what she was thinking.

"All right," I said. "Two telephone calls."

She brightened with relief. "Oh, thank you, Malia. You're so wonderful. Rachel is also climbing the walls in Jerusalem. Hearing your voice would do wonders for her as well. I'm sorry to ask you to do this, but I really appreciate it."

"Don't apologize, Mother," I said. "I want to make the calls. I just want to ask you one favor."

"Of course, Malia. Anything."

"Could you dial for me?"

A minute later I was holding the phone to my ear, listening to the distinctive hollow sound of a telephone ringing overseas. I heard the connection being made, and my grandfather's voice came on the line.

"Hallo," he said. "Who's speaking?"

"Zeidi!" I called out. "It's me. Malia!"

"Malia? Malia?" he repeated incredulously. "Is it really you?"

"It's really me, Zeidi."

"Oy, I thank the *Ribono shel Olam* to hear your voice. Tell me, *mein kind*, how are you feeling? What hurts you?"

I laughed. "I'm feeling pretty good. And nothing hurts me. I'm just feeling a little weak. Don't worry about me."

"'Don't worry about me'?" he mimicked. "Don't worry about you? My dear Malia'le, about whom should I worry right now if not you?

Don't tell me not to worry. I worry. I worry and I pray to Hashem that He should take care of you. Now I have to give the telephone to your Bubbi. She won't let me say another word. Good bye, Malia'le, and a *refuah sheleimah.*"

The sound of the telephone changing hands came across the lines, and then I heard my grandmother's agitated voice. "Malia'le, Malia'le, my poor little Malia'le, tell me how you are. Oy, please tell me everything."

"There's not so much to tell, Bubbi. I'm a little sick, and I have to get better."

"A little sick, you say? A little sick? Going to the hospital is more than a little sick. We are praying for you, Malia'le. Your Zeidi and I don't forget about you, not even for a minute. You're going to get well, with Hashem's help.Do you hear me?"

"I hear you, Bubbi."

"Good. Now, listen to me. Just because you're in the hospital and you have all those doctors and nurses around you doesn't mean that you don't have to take care of yourself. Do you understand me?"

"I'm not exactly sure, Bubbi." I had no inkling of what she meant.

"I mean that you have to take care of yourself. You have to make sure you get enough to eat and plenty of liquids to drink. Get lots of sleep. It's not so easy to sleep in a hospital, you know. There's so much noise, and people running around. Make sure you sleep. And you have to get exercise. Don't wait for them to take you for a walk. Do it yourself. You have to keep up your strength, okay?"

I smiled. "Now I understand, Bubbi. Thank you."

"Get well, *shaifeleh.* We love you, and we're praying for you. Good night."

"Good night, Bubbi."

I put down the telephone. Just a few minutes, and I was already exhausted. I closed my eyes for a minute and took a few deep breaths. Then I thought about Rachel and decided I could handle another few minutes.

"Would you like to call Rachel, Mother?" I said. "Just for a minute or two."

"Are you up to it?" she asked.

I nodded and closed my eyes. I felt a little dizzy.

Mother dialed quickly. She spoke into the telephone in low tones. I barely heard her. Finally, she got Rachel on the line and handed me the telephone.

"Malia!" Rachel shrieked across six thousand miles of space. "Malia! I can't stand it here! I feel so horrible to be here so far away from everything. You're my only sister, and I love you. I want to be with you. What kind of a terrible person am I to go away at a time like this?"

"Please, Rachel, don't be upset. You'll be home before you know it, and we'll be together. I'm okay. I really am."

"Okay? How can you say you're okay? You're sick, Malia. Really sick. And I'm scared out of my wits. I should be there with you. I should be sharing your experiences with you, but I'm on the other side of the world. People come over to me and congratulate me on my engagement, and I smile at them and thank them. But it's all a sham! Inside I'm crying, Malia. Inside, I'm sick with worry. Inside, I-I . . ." I heard her sobbing through the telephone, and I couldn't keep myself from joining her.

"Rachel, Rachel," I whispered when I got a little control of myself, "listen to me. I know that you love me, and that's what counts. It's just like you're here by my side. I'm going to write a book, Rachel, about everything that's happening to me. When you come back, you'll read it, and help me work on it. That way, you'll share everything I experienced from the beginning of this business. But for now, just be strong and enjoy the little time you have left in Jerusalem. Do it for me. It means a lot to me."

I heard her sniffle and quiet down. "All right, Malia. Just hang in there. I'll be home very soon. I pray for you all the time. I love you." She hung up before I could say another word. I suppose it was better than starting to cry all over again.

Reuven handed me a tissue. "You might need this, Malia," he said.

"Thanks," I said. I took the tissue and dabbed at the corners of my eyes.

Reuven glanced at his watch. "It's time for *Minchah*," he said. "I'm sorry, but I have to get going. Is there anything you'd like me to do?"

"Yes," I said, with a warm smile. "Take Mother home. She's been here since 8:00 in the morning."

"I don't want to leave," Mother protested. "I want to make sure you're okay." No matter how efficient and wonderful the nurses might be, I was still only one patient on a busy floor. Mother wanted me to have round-the-clock attention.

"I'll be okay, Mother," I said reassuringly. "Today's test went fine, and I don't start the chemo until tomorrow. You've been here every night since I came in, five days ago. Please go home and get a good night's sleep."

Mother argued a little more.

I gave her my most winsome smile. "If you really love me, Mother, you'll go home for one night."

Mother gave in. Reuven gave me a private wink as he ushered Mother out of the room. I stretched out in the bed, trying to relax. I was alone for the night. I was sure it would be fine.

About 2:00 in the morning, I awoke. I was feeling sick and weak. I closed my eyes and willed myself to doze off again, but the weakness and dizziness persisted. I pushed the button for the nurse and waited. No one came.

The minutes dragged by slowly. I fought down the rising feeling of panic as I pushed the button again and again. I wasn't strong enough to go to the door and call the nurse myself. All I could do was keep ringing the bell, hoping and praying that the nurse would come. But nothing happened.

Maybe the night nurse is on her rounds, I thought. Maybe she'll be back in a minute.

When the clock showed me that an agonizingly long hour had passed without any appearance by the nurse, I tremblingly lifted the phone and called my parents' home. Mother answered.

"Malia? What's wrong?"

"I'm so sorry, Mother," I whispered. "It's not an emergency, I'm okay, but the nurse doesn't come when I call. I'm afraid that if there is an emergency, Heaven forbid, there won't be anyone to help me."

"Don't say another word," Mother said soothingly. "Father will bring me right over."

In the middle of the night, it doesn't take too long to travel from Flatbush to Boro Park. Before I knew it, Mother was standing outside my door, scrubbing up and pulling on her mask before she came inside.

The night nurse was with her. "I'm so sorry, dear," she apologized as she came into the room together with Ma. "Please understand, all hospitals are understaffed at night. There isn't really an opportunity to check up on each patient individually. We count on seeing the light outside your room go on when you call us."

"So what happened?" I asked. It didn't matter that much now, since Mother was there.

The nurse spread out her hands. "Well, you see . . . your bulb burnt out!"

I couldn't help laughing in surprise. "I'm so glad we found out now," I said. "Will they fix it?"

"Of course they will," Mother said firmly. "But it doesn't matter, because I'll be staying here as long as you're in the hospital."

Mother was as good as her word. She brought a toothbrush, a change of clothing and a robe and put them in my locker. She obtained a special card giving her official permission to remain with me during non-visiting hours. Mr. Douglas Jablon, assistant to the president of the hospital, arranged for Mother to get a comfortable recliner where she could sleep right next to me. The Rivka Laufer Bikur Cholim organization sent us cake and coffee daily throughout our stay and provided us with a tiny refrigerator that fit into the corner of the room. With these and other little amenities, we were ready to face the coming month and the first round of chemotherapy which would, G-d willing, put me into remission.

On Chemotherapy

On Wednesday afternoon, Dr. Ruben performed a second bone marrow test. The doctors wanted to be able to compare my counts before and after the treatment. Once the test was completed, I was started on chemotherapy.

It was astonishing how quickly I learned the tongue-twisting names of the chemo drugs as well as the medications I took to counteract their side effects. Zofran and Atavan for nausea, Bentell and Karofate to line the stomach, Vancomycin to line the intestines, Prixamin, Lotrimin and Fortaz as antibiotics—and those were only the medicines I took to help me through the chemo! The chemotherapy itself consisted of two different drugs administered by IV, Idarubicin and Citarabin. Idarubicin was orange in color, so I dubbed it "orange punch," since it would punch away the bad cells.

Every time one of the drugs finished dripping through the IV, the nurses would flush the IV with heparin and saline to wash through the last drops of medication. The first time this was done, I had a strange, unpleasant taste in my mouth. After a while, I realized that I actually tasted the heparin. Eventually, I discovered that if I pinched my nose shut while the IV was being flushed, I wouldn't taste the heparin. I felt ridiculous, lying there holding my nose, but it worked.

One of the nurses saw what I was doing. "Aha!" she exclaimed. "So you're a heparin taster, too!" Apparently, I wasn't the only one.

The dedication of my doctors and nurses was incredible. Before I could get blood transfusions, I had to be premedicated. Then the specific numbers were checked and rechecked by two different nurses to make sure the blood was the proper type and cross match. Special filters needed to be connected. The chemotherapy drugs went through a special IV machine, computerized so that the right amount dripped into my system per minute. Blood pressure and temperature needed to be taken before and after every transfusion and treatment. And I was just one patient! I don't know how they managed!

My uncle Izzy, who owns a scarf business, sent me a dozen pretty scarves to "tip" the nice nurses. I was so glad to be able to present the dedicated staff with this little token of appreciation. They were all very moved by this gesture. These nurses work so hard, day in and day out, and just a little "thank you" is enough to make their day.

The nurses were really wonderful. They came to know us on a personal basis, sharing their lives with us. One nurse told us how she'd started in the pediatric ward and eventually switched to adult nursing. Another nurse, a Jewish woman whose husband wanted her to become religious, told us that if she'd met Mother and me twenty years ago, she would be religious today. We were both touched.

Strangely enough, things soon settled into a routine. Mother spent her nights half-dozing on the recliner chair next to my bed. Mrs. Borenstein, Gavriel's mother-in-law, also taught in Shulamith, and she drove Mother to school every morning. She always brought a thermos of hot coffee and a cheese danish so my mother could eat breakfast. By 8 a.m., Reuven would already be with me, having gone to an early *minyan* for *Shacharis*.

Reuven and I would spend the mornings together. The doctors had asked him and Mother to log everything that happened, so he was often scribbling down little details: fevers, medication, what I ate. Once, I managed to eat an entire apple. Reuven was delighted that I'd actually eaten something and wrote it down, adding a "smiley face" at the end of the sentence. Unfortunately, two lines later, he had to write, "Threw up apple," this time with a "sad face" at the end of the line. But at least we could laugh about it!

Reuven was anxious to do anything he could for me. Anything I asked for was "no problem!"

And if I didn't ask, he asked me. "Do you need anything? Hot water, cold water? Something from the store? The cafeteria? A book? A candy?"

If I ever actually had a craving for something to eat, such as ice cream, a hard-boiled egg or ices, he and Mother would drop everything in an effort to rush that food to me before my appetite was lost again.

Bubbi Rothman, Mother's mother, drove to Maimonides every single day with a delicious sandwich for Reuven's lunch. This was such a big favor for us, as this was the only food Reuven had to eat. She would knock quietly on the window in case I was asleep, then give Reuven the sandwich and me a *berachah* for a *refuah sheleimah*. She always prepared an extra sandwich, "just in case" I would have an appetite.

Mother would come back at about 2:30 in the afternoon, when she was finished teaching. Reuven would stay with us a little while longer, then go to *Minchah* and try to squeeze in a few hours of learning. He would return in the evening for another "hello" and to see how I was doing, staying until he had to leave to go to *Maariv*.

While he was there, if I had enough strength, we would call Monsey and talk to Dov on the phone. How I missed my children! I did my best to assure them they were wanted and missed. It made me glad to hear how happy he sounded, and, to listen to the little reports of what he'd done that day: swimming in the baby pool in the backyard or helping Bubbi Panzer bake cupcakes by putting on the sprinkles. At least I knew he and Ari were in loving hands. During the day, my married sisters-in-law took turns having Dov and Ari at their homes, feeding them and keeping them in good spirits.

Mother's best friends arranged shifts for sending supper for Mother, Reuven and me. The meals were prepared so beautifully, complete with silverware and tablecloth. It was too bad I couldn't eat any of it!

Father stopped by almost every day to visit me and to bring Mother fresh clothes. He had his hands full taking care of the house and doing all the laundry himself, but he was managing with a smile. He also brought all sorts of delicacies that he hoped would whet my appetite.

Zeidi Rothman, Mother's father, usually came by in the evenings. He couldn't come into the room, but he waved at us through the window so I would know he was thinking about me.

The day came to a close when Mother would call Father, Reuven and the Panzers in Monsey with a final report on how I was doing. Then we would try to settle in for another night of chemotherapy and (hopefully) sleep.

I spent most of the first three days of chemotherapy dozing. I simply had no energy for anything, including eating. All I could manage were soft foods like soup and applesauce. I experienced a strange side effect of the chemo: it made everything taste bitter, including water! Nonetheless, despite my inability to eat, I kept gaining weight. With all the liquids I was receiving through the IV, I was becoming terribly bloated. Within two weeks of my admission to the hospital, I had gained fourteen pounds!

At one point, when Mother was away teaching at school, I called the house. No one was home, and I got the answering machine. I didn't want to just hang up, so I sang onto the machine, "*Mitzvah gedolah lehiyos besimchah tamid.* It is a great *mitzvah* always to be cheerful." Father, the first one home that day, listened to the tape. He was so glad to hear me singing that he saved the tape and listened to it every single day!

On Thursday night, I began running a fever. Mother took my temperature and was alarmed to see that I had a fever of 104. When the nurse took my blood pressure, she saw it had dropped from the norm of 110/70 to 90/50. The end result was a blood transfusion that night and another on Friday. Thankfully, I did not need any blood products on Shabbos.

The chemotherapy continued. Although the fever persisted, all the blood tests produced negative results. Father, who had walked into Boro Park on Shabbos afternoon to sing *zemiros* for us and to tell us stories (Father is a great storyteller!), came back on Motzaei Shabbos to make *Havdalah* for Mother and me. Reuven had spent Shabbos in Monsey at my insistence. He wanted to stay with me, but I wanted my kids to be with their father! David brought us *melaveh malkah,* but the biggest treat for me was talking to Dov on the phone. It made me feel so much better to hear his cheerful voice over the wires.

The following day, the Panzers drove in from Monsey with the kids. Reuven came up and told me that Dov and Ari were there. "Do you want us to bring them up?" he asked.

I hesitated. It was really tempting, but I was unsure. "It's better if they don't," I said finally. "They can't come into the room, and it'll be too hard on them if they see their mommy but can't reach me. Besides, I'd rather not expose them to all the germs floating through the wards."

In the end, my children waited downstairs in the lobby while my in-laws came upstairs and waved to me through the window. I felt a rush of gratitude to Hashem for giving me such wonderful in-laws. They had taken my children with open arms, and they were willing to come all the way from Monsey just to wave through a window in a closed door. It was such a comfort to me to know that we had such strong support behind us.

As I lay in bed, watching the drugs drip through the IV, I was struck with a sudden sense of wonder. I was so grateful to Hashem for granting mankind the wisdom to develop the medications to counteract a disease like leukemia. And I was also thankful that these cures were developed before my time!

On Monday, Dr. Grinberg came by. He was one of the five doctors in the ward. Like Dr. Kopel, Dr. Bashevkin, and Dr. Ruben, Dr. Grinberg had given Mother his personal phone number, so we could reach him whenever necessary.

"Malia, you're doing okay," he said with approval as he checked my chart. He smiled underneath his mask. "I don't usually say anything complimentary, because I don't like discharging patients so early, but you're doing superbly!"

As he left the room, Mother and I looked at each other and chuckled. We knew I wasn't leaving yet, but it was funny anyway. I was glad my doctors were such friendly people.

That afternoon, my sister-in-law brought me a VCR and some tapes so I shouldn't get bored. Mother was about to plug it in when one of the nurses stopped her.

"You can't plug that in yourself!" she exclaimed.

Mother suddenly looked alarmed. "Why not? Can a VCR damage the medical equipment?"

"It's not that," the nurse said, shaking her head. "The hospital engineer has to do it for you."

Mother was bewildered. "An engineer? All you have to do is put the plug in the socket!"

"I'm sorry," the nurse said firmly. "I'll call the engineer right away, and he'll take care of it."

Sure enough, within half an hour, the engineer showed up. Mother showed him the VCR, and he plugged it into the wall. Such excitement for such a simple task!

"Just hospital procedure," I told Mother. "The special IV nurse is the only one who can start my IV, too!" Once the IV was in, of course, any nurse could give me medication.

The chemotherapy continued, and so did the fevers. The doctors tried antibiotic after antibiotic. At one point, Monica, one of my nurses, gave me a small bag of antibiotics called Fortaz through the IV. The only problem was the tiny hole in the tubing. About a quarter of the fluid spilled out, so it took only five minutes or so to drip in.

I rang the bell. Monica came in and saw the limp bag hanging on the IV pole. "What?" she said, surprised. "It's already finished?"

"There's a hole in the tubing, dear Monica, a hole," I sang to her. She took a good look and burst out laughing.

"Just keep up the good spirits, Malia!" she said as she went to get fresh tubing.

As the days passed, my wall grew increasingly crowded. Friends and relatives continued to send me cards and posters. Moshe sent a beautiful banner he'd designed in his yeshivah in Philadelphia. My favorite card was from my aunt's sister-in-law, who wrote, "When you start making bad jokes and awful puns, you'll know you have our blood!" We had no flowers in the room, since they can harbor germs; if anyone ever brought a bouquet as a gift, we either sent it to other wards or gave it to our next guest.

I couldn't believe the number of people who came to visit. They all knew they wouldn't be able to actually come inside the room; all they could do was stand by the window and wave. Despite this, many people came again and again, especially Dr. Shapiro, Dr. Mann, my obstetrician, and my parents' friends, Dr. and Dr. Shulman. They had their own patients and families, but they still came and checked up on me.

David had gone back to Israel, but before he left, he gave us two priceless gifts. The first was a makeshift curtain for my window, so I could have a few minutes of privacy when I desperately needed it; for example, when I was throwing up. I didn't particularly care for an audience at times like that. He also gave us a beeper for Mother, so she could keep in touch with a few important people and avoid the rest of the phone calls that were constantly coming in.

Poor Father. With Mother in the hospital and unable to field the calls, he spent hours and hours on the phone, patiently listening to the dogmatic opinions of the dozens of considerate, well-meaning people who had our best interests in mind and generally drove him crazy. "Why aren't you using that hospital? . . . you should leave Maimonides immediately and go to Manhattan . . . don't ever do . . . you shouldn't listen to *that* doctor . . . she would do better on this diet, the one that would *really* save her life . . . and don't even think about macrobiotics . . ." The pressure grew so extreme that Reuven, who was also bombarded by such conversations from all sides, eventually switched to a different *shul* where he wasn't so well known. He simply could not bear yet another demand as to why we were not doing the one thing that would surely save my life.

Reuven and I, as well as Mother and Father, were not interested in these phone calls and assertions. While we appreciated the concern behind these opinions, we were extremely satisfied with Maimonides Hospital. We all felt secure with our excellent doctors and the dedicated nursing staff. A person has to help himself as much as possible, but in the end, even the "best" of doctors are merely Hashem's messengers. We were confident that Hashem could find messengers even outside of Manhattan!

Others, instead of trying to meddle into my treatments, offered prayers for my recovery. Zeidi Greenberg, in Israel, went to the Western Wall daily to pray on my behalf. Bubbi Greenberg, who has trouble walking, was unable to make the daily trip from Bayit Vegan to the Old City, but she poured her heart and soul into her *Tehillim* at home. She had a ruby, a heirloom from the daughter of the Baal Shem Tov that if worn by a sick person can be a *segulah* for recovery. She immediately sent it to America, and it hung around my neck throughout my entire ordeal.

Zeidi Greenberg does not often remember his dreams, so he takes his dreams very seriously when he does. Shortly after Rachel told him what was wrong with me, he dreamed he saw a *pasuk* of *Chumash* that compares the weight of blood to the meat of an animal. The following morning, he called America to find out exactly how much I weigh. When he heard I weighed one hundred and twenty-six pounds, he went to a butcher, asked him to weigh out one hundred and twenty-six pounds worth of meat, and gave that amount of money to charity in my behalf! He felt sure the merit of this *mitzvah* would help me have a speedy recovery. He also sent me oil from the gravesite of Rabbi Shimon bar Yochai in Miron, which is also considered a *segulah* for recovery. I didn't know where to put it, so I rubbed it on the bone marrow test site, since all the blood cells are produced in the bone marrow.

A friend of Mother's in Toronto sent me the handwritten manuscript of the Kesav Sofer, which I took along with me when I was admitted. An uncle, who records *Daf Yomi* tapes, dedicated every tape he made during this period for my recovery. We knew that our friends and relatives offered prayers daily on my behalf. With such strong spiritual support, how could we not remain optimistic?

Tuesday was the last day of chemo. Dr. Nawabi, the head of the department, scrubbed up and entered the room. He examined my chart and nodded his approval.

"Well done, Malia! How are you feeling?"

"Fine, but I'm itching a lot," I admitted. "My skin is getting blotchy, too."

Dr. Nawabi took a good look. "It might be a yeast infection. That's a common reaction to strong antibiotics."

He sent Dr. Fastman to check me, and he agreed. I was started on yet another medication to fight the yeast infection.

"Don't worry, Malia," Dr. Fastman assured me. "This will clear up soon enough, and you'll soon be on the way to recovery!"

"*B'ezras Hashem,*" I replied.

I had confidence that Hashem would make things work out.

The End of Stage One

On Wednesday, I had three doctors in attendance as I was taken off the chemo. I had no pipes, no tubes, nothing attached to me. I felt free for the first time in a week! I was practically dancing around the room.

"Hooray!" I yelled. "I can move my arms!"

Reuven grinned. "You're doing great, Malia!" he exclaimed. He turned to Dr. Grinberg. "So what's the next step, doctor?"

"Now we wait," Dr. Grinberg replied. "Malia's white blood count is extremely low right now. She's very susceptible to infection. Once her counts go back up, we can think about a complete cure." He smiled. "It's good to see an optimistic patient. If you keep this up, Malia, you'll be in complete remission in no time at all. You're really doing well."

"Terrific," I said happily. Even though I still had that persistent fever, I felt wonderful. I even managed to eat something that day! Usually, whatever went down came right back up. "The opposite of the law of gravity," Mother joked tiredly. She, too, was eating poorly. As she put it, "How can I eat when Malia can't even keep down a sip of water?"

Bubbi Rothman came by that day to visit me, as she did every day. She brought me sweet-smelling spices in the spice box that belonged to the holy Rabbi Nachum of Chernobyl, urging me to make a *berachah*. I was struck by the thought that I used to visit her daily with the children, but that seemed like another lifetime. My new life had hospital beds and intravenous tubes and doctors and nurses and fear and, yes, hope. Always hope.

Thursday was day nine since the chemotherapy had begun. The doctors had warned me that days ten through fourteen of the cycle were the most difficult in terms of weakness, since I would be cytopenic, or very low in white blood cells. Sure enough, I found myself so weak I could barely move, even though it was a day early. I comforted myself with the reminder that this would last only a few days before I began to recover my strength. At least my "orange punch" had destroyed all the leukemic cells!

At 11:00 in the morning, Dr. Ruben scrubbed up and donned his mask before coming into the room.

"There's somebody here today, Malia," he told me. "Her name is Anne-Marie Geraldo. She's here with her mother. She's also twenty-two years old, and she had leukemia a year ago. She's fine now. She's willing to meet with you, if you'd like."

Someone my age, who had been through this same ordeal? "Oh, yes!" I exclaimed. "Please. I'd really like to talk to her."

"I'll bring her, then," Dr. Ruben said, turning to go.

I felt so grateful. My doctors weren't only concerned with facts and statistics. They were doing everything they could, in every way possible, to make me feel better about the situation.

Anne-Marie and her mother arrived a few minutes later. Reuven left the room so we could have some "women talk." We sat and talked for about half an hour. Anne-Marie had gone through an autologous bone marrow transplant. In other words, since they were unable to find a match, they harvested her own bone marrow, bombarded it with extremely high doses of chemo and radiation, and then put the cleansed marrow back into her system. She was completely cured.

After a while, Mother rose and suggested that Anne-Marie and I have a chance to talk alone. After Mother left, I haltingly asked Anne-Marie about some of my most private fears. In particular, I was worried about coping with the pain of the treatments I would have to face and also about the possibility of not being able to have more children.

Anne-Marie's face was serious as she answered my questions. "Pain is subjective, of course," she told me. "Some people say the spinal tap is the worst. Others say the reaction to the chemo and the other medications is the hardest. Some people can't handle the nausea, or the bone marrow tests, or the terrible mouth sores. Some women find the hair loss most difficult to cope with. It all depends on you. I personally had a great deal of trouble with my liver. But everyone is different."

"And having children?" I asked, almost afraid to hear an answer. Anne-Marie was an Italian, not a religious Jew like me. Could she understand how important this was to me?

Anne-Marie sighed. "They say that after a bone marrow transplant, it's not possible anymore," she said quietly. "The radiation destroys the ability to have children. I know one woman who had four boys before she had her transplant. She'd always wanted a girl, but now it was impossible. She told me that she really appreciates her children now." She paused. "Do you have any children?"

"Yes," I whispered. "Two boys." My eyes went to the studio photographs on the wall.

Anne-Marie followed my gaze. "Two beautiful boys," she said soberly. "Appreciate them, Malia. Be grateful that you married young and already have sons of your own. If you only need chemotherapy, there's a possibility that you'll still be able to have children, but if you need a transplant . . ." Her voice trailed off. I could almost hear her adding, "and most people do." I could sense her sadness at being deprived of the prospect of motherhood. My heart went out to her.

I was silent for a moment. "Thank you for telling me," I said at last.

No one knows the future. No one knows what Hashem has in store for him or her. Anne-Marie was right; I had to acknowledge and appreciate the wonderful gift of my two sons. With Hashem's help, if a bone marrow transplant proved unnecessary, perhaps I would have more children, but I had to face the possibility that I might never have another child.

"Of course," Anne-Marie added after another short silence, "G-d can always make miracles."

We talked a little longer, then Anne-Marie left. I was pretty quiet the rest of the day. She had given me a lot to think about. The most important thing, I decided, was to concentrate on how Anne-Marie was now healthy and well. Hair loss, pain, all these things paled beside the truly important goal: life. The first step was to beat the leukemia. I would let Hashem worry about whether or not I would be able to have more children. As Anne-Marie had said, Hashem can always make miracles if He so desires.

That afternoon, I threw up again. The ever-present nausea, together with the fever that refused to go away, just wouldn't let me keep anything down. At midnight, I was retching horribly, and I threw up green bile. That frightened me. Anne-Marie had said she had trouble with her liver. Was that happening to me, too, Heaven forbid?

Mother called Carmen, the nurse on duty, who reassured me that my liver was okay. "You have nothing left in your system," she explained sympathetically. "That's why you're vomiting bile."

The long night continued. Mother was up with me the entire time, just holding my hand. At 6:00 in the morning, I was still retching. Now I spit up some blood. That frightened me again. This time, Carmen explained, "You've scratched your esophagus from all the vomiting, Malia. I know it's not pleasant, but try not to worry. It's not a sign of anything seriously wrong."

We finally made it to Friday morning. That had been the hardest night so far. I only prayed to Hashem that it should be the worst of it.

One of the nurses' aides, Miss Sargent, came to check on me that morning. She saw that I looked drained, weak and miserable.

"Let me help you, honey," she offered. "How about if I wash your hair?"

I had no energy to do such a thing myself. She gently washed my hair, and I did feel much better. It was so sweet of her to do this for me even though it wasn't part of her job. She cared about me and wanted me to feel fresh and clean.

It was time for my first platelet transfusion. Until now, I'd only received blood. All the doctors on the team came to check me before the transfusion began.

As soon as the platelets began to enter my system, I began to shiver all over. I had the chills, and nothing seemed to warm me. The nurses rubbed me and covered me with blankets, but it took a long twenty minutes before I finally felt warm enough to calm down.

"We won't let it happen again," Dr. Ruben promised. "We'll pre-medicate you with Demerol before your next transfusion of platelets."

"Whatever it takes," I said. The reaction was over now. I lifted my chin and smiled at Mother and Reuven. We were going to see this through!

Shabbos came. Again, Father walked from Flatbush so he could join us in the afternoon for *zemiros* and stories, while Reuven stayed with Dov and Ari in Monsey. We had an unexpected addition to the *zemiros* when a "singing" card taped to the wall fell open. The card played the same tinny tune, over and over. We looked at each other, laughing helplessly. There was nothing we could do except hope that the tiny battery would eventually run out.

Looking back, I find that we laughed at so many things that seem quite silly now. I think we laughed to keep ourselves from crying.

About five minutes after the music started, Theresa came into the room. "Hi, I have to take your blood pressure," she said cheerfully. She looked around for the source of the music and grimaced. "Hey, do you like that musical thing?"

"No," said Mother.

"Then why are you listening to it?"

"Because we can't shut it."

"Oh, because it's Shabbos, right?" she asked.

"That's right," Mother replied.

"Well, it's a good thing I showed up!" she exclaimed. She taped the card closed very tightly and hung it back on the wall. "That should take care of it." She chuckled and left the room.

Two weeks passed. I was still receiving blood and platelets transfusions, still waiting for my white blood count to go up to normal levels. And the fevers kept persisting.

By now, the doctors had ruled out every other possible source of fever except a fungus infection. "If the fever doesn't go down in the next day or two, we'll have to give her Enfetericin," Dr. Kopel told Reuven.

"What's wrong with Enfetericin?" Reuven asked.

Dr. Kopel smiled ruefully through his mask. "It's a very powerful antibiotic. But we only use it as a last resort because it has many side effects."

"What kind of side effects?" Reuven asked, a little anxious.

"Let's just put it this way," said Dr. Kopel. "Some people call it Enfeterrible."

The days of *Sefiras HaOmer* were passing by. Even though I had lost complete track of time, I still managed to count every night with a *berachah*. I had Reuven to thank for that! Father had told me that under the circumstances, I was certainly allowed to listen to music to keep up my spirits, but I felt better keeping the regular custom by listening to music during *Sefirah*. This was no easy thing for me, as I love music and I always had music playing on my kitchen tape recorder at home.

Lag BaOmer, the day of *Sefirah* when everyone listens to music, fell on a Motzaei Shabbos, twenty-two days after I'd first come to the hospital. Dr. Mann, my obstetrician, called Madeline, the head nurse, and asked for permission to bring somebody into the hospital to play live music for us.

"Of course," Madeline agreed. "Anything that will keep Malia in good spirits is worthwhile."

Mother and I knew nothing of this. I was on the phone with Reuven in Monsey, asking how his Shabbos had been with the children. Suddenly, at 10:00 at night, Dr. Mann came into my room, followed by a very talented musician from Russia. I watched in disbelief as the two of them sat down, masked and scrubbed, and the musician began to play beautiful Russian songs on his accordion. It was too much for me, and for Mother, too. My emotional bubble burst, and I wept for the first time since I'd come into the hospital. I don't know if I can ever thank Dr. Mann enough for this wonderful gesture. It was so thoughtful and brought so much comfort to my hospital stay.

The next day, my doctors decided to put me on Enfetericin. They'd removed the central line to check if it was infected, so I had to get the IV in my arm again. Dr. Plantilla came in to replace the central line right after I was hooked up to the Enfetericin. After this one dose, he told me, I would go back to the central line and get my transfusions without pain.

Just as he was finishing up with the stitches, I started to shake. I couldn't help myself. I knew I had to lie motionless while he finished sewing, but I was trembling so violently that it was all he could do to sew the last stitch. Mother once again piled blankets on me. Then she, Reuven and two nurses rubbed me as hard as they could to warm me up. Dr. Wolnitz, the house doctor, and Madeline, the head nurse, also came into the room to make sure I was all right. It seemed to take much longer than it actually did, but the shakes finally stopped.

"I'll tell Dr. Kopel," Dr. Wolnitz told me. "From now, we're going to premedicate you before starting anything new."

"Good," I said with a weak smile. I appreciated Dr. Wolnitz's concern. She was always smiling, always caring about her patients on the floor.

The shakes weren't the only reaction I got from the "Enfeterrible." Bad as my nausea had been before, it was now much worse. Enfetericin also drains potassium from the body, so

I was given K-riders, both through shots and the IV. But since injections of potassium into the body can cause an extra strain on the heart, I also had to be monitored by a cardiac machine. Mother, watching this all happen, said wryly, "I wonder what *my* EKG would look like now?"

Still, I couldn't complain. At least the fevers were finally gone.

"You're doing well, Malia," Dr. Grinberg said one day as he checked my lungs for the umpteenth time. "But you have to start getting some exercise to keep your lungs fully expanded. I know you're weak and tired, but try walking around the room a little whenever you find enough strength."

I knew it was for my own good, so I walked back and forth in my little room whenever I could. I found it very exhausting, but I was determined to do the best I could to help myself get better.

The first time I got out of bed, I took one look at my feet and had another laughing jag. I'd become so badly bloated and swollen that it looked like I had two ankles instead of one on each foot! I was laughing so hard I couldn't tell Mother what was funny. Finally, I just pointed to my feet. She gave me a rueful smile. "I'm glad you can laugh about it," she said.

After a few days, I could feel my strength slowly returning. The doctors gave me permission to start taking walks in the hall. "You'll have to wear a mask," Dr. Kopel explained. "You're still very susceptible to germs."

"No problem," I said, beaming. The prospect of actually getting out of my little room made anything worthwhile!

It felt strange to walk down the hallway with Mother at my side. All the nurses turned to me with cheerful hellos, but it took an effort to recognize them. It was the first time I was seeing them without their masks.

At about the same time, I found myself coping with a new ordeal—hair loss. The doctors had explained that chemotherapy, while destroying the leukemic cells, also destroys good cells in the intestines as well as the hair cells. Somehow, though, I had assumed it wouldn't happen to me.

Then I woke up one morning and saw hairs on my pillow. I realized that it was actually going to happen. The sight of great clumps of hair coming loose every time I brushed my hair gave me a sick feeling in the pit of my stomach. As if I needed another sign that my illness was very real! As a woman, I also found it hard to deal with the loss of my hair. Would I become completely bald, like Rose Scheiner? Would it grow back after I recovered? But then I decided to look at the bright side. Some people lose all their hair at once, but my hair was so thick that I was losing it gradually. I would have time to adjust. Thank Heaven for small favors.

Reuven suggested I get a short haircut before my hair fell out; it would be less traumatic. I agreed. Mother's friend Lèlè, an expert wigmaker, came and cut my hair, being extra careful with the scissors since it was so dangerous for me to bleed. She also bought a short wig for me and styled it. I was grateful to Reuven for his brilliant idea, which certainly made things easier when the hair loss really started getting bad. Besides, as a religious Jewish married woman, I always cover my hair either with a wig or a kerchief. If this is so difficult for me, I thought, how much more traumatic this must be for a woman who does not ordinarily cover her hair.

Three weeks had already passed in the hospital.

On Thursday, the doctors gave me a water pill, Aldectone, to drain the excess fluids from my body. It was astonishing how quickly it worked. By Friday afternoon, between the walking and the water pill, I'd already lost three and a half pounds.

Shabbos arrived, my fourth in the hospital. Reuven was in Monsey again, with Dov and Ari. About half an hour after candle lighting, some of my favorite visitors arrived at the door: Mr. Brandwein and his four young sons. Together, they stood at the door and called through the vents, "Good Shabbos. We hope that you have a speedy recovery." These people didn't even know us, but they came every single Shabbos to call out the same greeting at our closed door. What an incredible upbringing this man was giving his children!

The following morning, Calvin came by with his friendly smile to take a finger prick for my blood results. "How are you doing today?" he boomed at me.

"Fine," I said.

He waved a friendly hand and went to take the results down to the lab. Dr. Kopel came into the room a little while later, whistling under his breath as he always did.

"Good news, Malia!" he exclaimed. "You have over five hundred neutrophils!"

"That's great," I said, "but what does it mean?"

Mother, who had learned a great deal in the past month, already knew. "That means Malia has enough white blood cells to fight infection, doesn't it?"

"Yes," Dr. Kopel said. "Much as we'd like to keep you here, it looks like we're going to have to let you go. Stage one is coming to an end."

"You mean . . . go home?" I felt dazed. It didn't seem like such a thing was possible.

"Would you rather stay?" he joked. He turned to go. "We'll have a more definite picture later in the day."

Sure enough, I soon got confirmation: I could go home the following day. I would have four weeks at home in which to recover my strength before the next step was taken in completely destroying the leukemia in my body. I was so excited! I couldn't believe it was true!

We called Reuven as soon as Shabbos was over, and he rushed back from Monsey to help us pack. As he and Mother started getting my things together, I was taken aback at the number of things we'd accumulated over the past month. Robes, kerchiefs, socks, slippers. All the crackers and candies Reuven had brought, hoping I would eat. Dozens of books, games, gifts. Just taking down the decorations on the wall took hours! We had to arrange for the little refrigerator to go back to the Bikur Cholim society, and Mother's recliner had to be returned. The VCR had to go back to my sister-in-law. Reuven kept busy, trotting back and forth between my room and his car, trying to get everything packed so I could leave in the morning.

After six trips down the elevator and out of the hospital to the car, juggling five bags each time, Reuven made his last trip with the VCR. As he approached the entrance, the guard stopped him.

"Where are you going with all that stuff?" he asked gruffly but with a distinct twinkle in his eye. "You're packing out the whole Maimonides, and now you're taking our computers, too?"

"My wife is going home," Reuven explained. It was one of the sweetest sentences he had ever uttered.

No Place Like Home

I walked out of the hospital doors slowly, savoring each step. Just outside, I stopped for a moment to take a good, deep breath. Fresh air. A cool breeze. How I had missed the outdoors during the long month spent in the confines of that sterile little room in K-5!

Reuven, standing next to me, looked concerned. "Okay?" he asked.

"Very," I replied with feeling.

As we walked to the car, I kept taking deep, deep breaths. It was a marvelous spring day, with the kind of weather that lends a sparkle to the air. Thank You, Hashem, I thought gratefully, for making my homecoming day so beautiful.

Reuven settled me into the back seat of the car with a pillow comfortably cushioning my head. Soon, we turned out of the hospital drive and started home.

"Slow down, Reuven," I gasped, clutching at the door handle. "You're going much too fast!"

Reuven, surprised, pressed his foot on the brake. "I'm only going thirty-five," he said apologetically.

"I guess my reflexes are in slow motion. Drive a little more slowly, okay?"

"No problem."

I smiled to myself. Reuven had used that same expression throughout the entire month at the hospital.

I sat by the open window, enjoying the feel of the wind on my face. I felt a strange kind of wonder at the scenes that flashed at me from the street. We were driving right through the heart of Boro Park, and the sidewalks were filled with people: girls walking together in animated groups, mothers shepherding groups of lively children into pizza shops, people shopping, talking, boys riding bicycles. All of it seemed so terribly, terribly . . . normal. For me, time had stopped for four long weeks, but to the outside world, nothing had happened.

Would I begin to take all of this for granted after a little while? I hoped not. I prayed Hashem would help me continue to value the beauty of the outdoor world and the marvel of being able to lead a normal life. I hoped, too, that I would never forget the kindness of the hundreds of people who had touched our lives, doctors and nurses, acquaintances, relatives, friends. I prayed I would always value every "little" thing done for me—the flowers, cards, pictures or posters. And of course, the big things—the people who had prayed ceaselessly for my recovery.

As Reuven turned off the main road, I told myself that the greatest gift to appreciate was life itself. I remembered one person who had spoken to me in the hospital. She, too, had been diagnosed with leukemia. When she was first cured, she was so happy to be alive that each day had been filled with the glow of appreciation. But as time passed, she grew so accustomed to her good health that she expected each day to be regular and normal.

I didn't want that to happen to me. I didn't ever want to be "normal" again. I wanted to take this appreciation and say to myself every day, "Wow! What a wonderful gift Hashem has given me today. I'm alive and well! I can walk. I can eat. I can care for my children by myself!" I didn't want to just take life as it comes any more. I wanted to savor each moment for the precious gift it is.

As we turned onto my parents' block, I put these reflections aside. Such thoughts were for the future, when I might find it difficult to hold onto the happiness and appreciation that came so easily to me today. For now, my joy at the prospect of being home again was enough to make me want to dance and sing, right then and there!

We pulled into the driveway. How wonderful to be home! My spirits soared as high as the blue sky overhead. Mother settled me in a lawn chair on the back porch. I sat quietly and listened to the birds twittering in the trees. I hadn't heard that delightful sound in a long, long time.

No one let me do anything. Reuven, Mother and Father were determined to see me rest as much as possible, so I would have enough strength for the next stage of our battle against my leukemia. For now, I was more than willing to comply. It was enough just to be within the beloved four walls of this house, curled up on the super-comfortable couch in the living room.

The first night I came home, a friend of mine, Bayla, came to visit me. She had called me many times during my hospital stay. She had also had leukemia, and she was willing to discuss it with me if I wanted to do so. Until now, I hadn't been ready to face the prospect of getting very deeply into someone else's story; it would have been too overwhelming. Even Anne-Marie's short visit, much as I had wanted it, had been terribly draining, both physically and emotionally. Now, though, I was ready to listen.

Bayla and I talked for over four hours. She hadn't spoken about her illness to anyone else until now, but she knew that I wasn't asking out of curiosity; I was asking for help. It was difficult emotionally for her to discuss her hard times, but she did it for me. It gave me such encouragement to see someone that had gone through the same ordeal and was cured. Bayla was healthy, alive and vibrant. I felt encouraged.

The following morning, Reuven asked, "What would you like to do today, Malia?" He meant it as a joke. I wasn't supposed to do anything except try to eat and rest. But I instantly replied, "Let's go see the kids!"

Reuven was sympathetic. He realized how much I longed to see my two precious little boys.

"Not just yet, Malia," he said gently. "Give yourself a couple of days to recuperate. I don't think you really understand how weak you are. I'm going to bring them back from Monsey on Friday, and we'll all have Shabbos together."

"But—" I started to protest.

"Malia, you wouldn't want them to come and find you with no strength to even pick up Ari."

I sighed and capitulated. Reuven was right, but I would find the wait impossibly long.

On Wednesday, I banged my foot against the edge of a chair. By nightfall, I had a huge black-and-blue mark. Reuven spotted it and looked worried.

"What happened? What fell on your foot?"

"Nothing," I reassured him. "It was just a little knock."

"A little knock?" he said incredulously.

I shrugged. "I guess it's the low platelets. It'll probably take ages to heal."

I was right about that one. That little bang against the chair left a bruise that lasted over a week.

Friday morning finally arrived, and Reuven left straight for Monsey to pick up the children. I found that I couldn't sit still. I was going to see my children! It had been five agonizingly long weeks since I'd seen them last. I kept running to look out the window. Maybe they were pulling into the driveway now. Maybe Dov was running up the steps. What would he say when he saw me? How would he react? On the phone he had been great, always sounding cheerful, always saying *"Refuah sheleimah!"* with a little prompting from his Bubbi Panzer. But what would he do now? And how would I react? And Ari, precious little Ari, to whom I hadn't even been able to talk—how can you speak to an infant?—what would happen when he saw me? Would I burst into tears? Would he recognize me at all?

My muddled thinking was suddenly interrupted. I heard Mother yell, "Malia, they're here!" I ran out of the house and gave Dov the biggest hug in the world! He hugged me back and gave me a kiss on the cheek before he said, "Mommy, I love you and I missed you so much!" I'd never heard nicer words in my life.

Then Reuven was holding Ari out to me. I took my baby boy and squeezed him tightly. How he had changed, going from five to six months old! And he was so cute. I couldn't tell if he remembered me or not, but it didn't really matter. He was happy and smiling at me. Much as I had missed my children in the hospital, it wasn't until now that I realized how much I had really longed to see them. At last, the four of us were a family again.

I played with Dov and Ari the entire Shabbos. Dov wanted to be near me at all times. He pushed his chair next to mine during meals and slept on the floor next to my bed. He cuddled close against me as I read him stories and beamed with delight when I gave him rides in his little car. Ari seemed content with the world as long as I held him in my arms.

I still tired easily. I realized that Reuven had been right to wait a few more days before bringing the children home. When I felt too exhausted to continue, I told Dov that the doctor said I had to rest. "You can sit with me here on the couch," I offered, and he was more than happy with this compromise.

When Shabbos ended, I was so drained I could barely move. But it had been worth it. What a wonderful, amazing miracle they are! I couldn't thank Hashem enough for the precious gift He had given me—my two little boys.

All too soon it was time for Reuven to take them back to Monsey. Their things were packed and stored in the car. I had to say goodbye.

"Mommy still has a boo-boo," I explained to Dov as I held him close. "You're going to go back to Bubbi Panzer while I get better."

"Can't I stay with you?" he asked.

"When I feel better, I'm going to come visit you in Monsey," I promised. "Now, are you going to be a good boy and help Bubbi Panzer take care of Ari?"

"Okay, Mommy," Dov said.

"You precious little boy," I whispered as I kissed him again. Thank Heaven, he was going back to Monsey in good spirits. I could continue to recuperate with peace of mind.

I took my recuperation seriously. I knew I couldn't just sit back and wait for my strength to come back by itself. I needed physical therapy, and I decided to get a very good physical therapist. Me.

First, I took stock of where I needed help. I needed to get some real nourishment into my body. I needed exercise to rebuild my atrophied muscles. And I needed fresh air for my body and for my soul.

Very wisely, I thought, I devised a steady but careful exercise program. Little by little I would work my way up to normal levels of exercise.

The first day, I walked up and down the driveway of my parents' house. I used to run up that driveway in one or two bounding strides, but now, navigating its entire length was a challenge and an adventure.

There was a white wrought-iron bench near the sidewalk, and I told myself I would not sit down on it unless I absolutely had to. I'm proud to say I didn't sit on it, although I was sorely tempted more than once to plop down and catch my breath.

The next day, I ventured out onto the sidewalk. It was a daring move, and it thrilled me to the bone. I felt like a Viking setting off across the uncharted ocean. I walked past my neighbor's house and thought about turning back. But my adventurous spirit prevailed, and I continued past one more house. That was enough! I turned around and walked back toward the house, placing one foot carefully before the other. This time, I rewarded my exertions with a few minutes on the bench.

The following day, I really ventured far into the wild blue yonder. I walked all the way to the corner and back. It was a major journey, and I had to get into bed when I returned home. But I was exhilarated. I was making progress!

My successes emboldened me, and the next day, I decided to round the corner and perhaps reach the next corner, which was only a short block away. I decided to take it slowly and carefully, not to push the outer limits of my endurance. I was a little nervous about the new plan, but I was confident I could pull it off.

The adventure began well. It was a beautiful day. The sun shone gently, and a soft breeze caressed my face. I felt brave and invigorated, and I got to the corner in high spirits. I turned the corner with a purposeful although deliberate stride and set my eyes on the next corner off in the distant horizon. I felt great, but only for another minute or two. By the time I passed the fourth house, my head was spinning and my left side was cramping up. I was all alone, too far from home to go back.

I looked up at the porch of the house on my right and saw a stone bench. I had no idea who lived in that house, but I knew that the bench was my only chance. With a great effort, I struggled up the path and climbed the three steps to the porch.

To my delight, there were a few outdoor cushions on the other side of the bench. I arranged them and sat down to rest.

I wondered who lived in that house. Would they be upset if they saw me, a perfect stranger, sitting there? I looked at the front door and saw a *mezuzah*, and I felt a sense of relief. I was sure I would receive only kindness from the owners of this house if I should happen to meet them while I rested on their bench. It even occurred to me that I might actually know them. Perhaps they even prayed in our *shul*. I tried to conjure up in my mind a picture of the lady of the house. I made her tall and slender and dressed her in a gray suit with a single strand of pearls at her neck. And I gave her the most beautiful smile.

After twenty minutes, I felt much better, strong enough to attempt the return journey. I never did get to meet my tall, slender hostess, but I am very grateful to her nonetheless.

Full Speed Ahead

11

A week after coming home, I had an appointment with Dr. Kopel. Not knowing what issues would arise nor what decisions would have to be made, I asked Mother and Reuven to accompany me.

As always, Dr. Kopel was clear and forthright in his explanations. "You know by now that cancer is an abnormal multiplication of certain cells," he began. "In your case, immature white blood cells have multiplied rapidly and crowded out the healthy cells in your bone marrow. The good news is that we've completed the cytogenic test taken on your first bone marrow test slides, and we now know you have APL, Acute Prolycytic Leukemia, which is a subtype of AML, Acute Myogenous Leukemia, which is what we originally assumed you had. AML is much more common."

"What does that mean, and what's the difference?" Reuven asked.

"The difference lies in the stage of development of those immature white blood cells," Dr. Kopel explained. "With APL, the cells are slightly more mature than they are in AML. This is excellent news, as there is a much greater success rate with APL than with AML."

"Am I going to need a bone marrow transplant?" I asked, steeling myself for his answer.

"Not necessarily. This is one of the advantages of APL." He looked pleased. "APL has an 85 percent chance of a total cure, using only high doses of chemotherapy. We may be able to cure you completely without a transplant."

I took a deep breath and let it out slowly. It had never occurred to me that I might avoid the transplant. As for the "85 percent chance," that was great, but I firmly believe that everyone's fate is in the hands of Hashem regardless of the statistical probabilities. You can't despair if the odds are against you, and you can't be complacent if the odds are in your favor.

"Of course, we have to be prepared for the possibility of a transplant," Dr. Kopel continued. "Your numbers should be high enough next week to be tested. As long as the immature cells are filling your bone marrow, we can't determine exactly what type of bone marrow you have. Once your numbers are close to normal, we can test you and your family to see if there's a match. I understand that some of your siblings have already been tested?"

I nodded. David and Gavriel had both given blood to be tested before they left. David had been positive he would be a perfect match! Rachel hadn't been tested, but she was due home the following week.

"All right, then. You'll go into Manhattan next week with the rest of your siblings and have blood drawn for testing." He smiled. "One more little piece of good news. We were able to locate the exact chromosomal imbalance. That means that a simple blood test will be able to warn us if there's a relapse, Heaven forbid."

"Heaven forbid," we all echoed simultaneously.

"For now, let's just concentrate on making a decision as to what our next step will be." Dr. Kopel leaned back in his chair and whistled a few bars before he added, "I would prefer to attempt the high doses of chemotherapy. The transplant is always an option if the chemo fails. However, I would seriously suggest that you go for a second opinion before you make your final decision. I recommend that you speak to Dr. Ellen Berman at Sloan-Kettering in

Manhattan. Sloan-Kettering specializes in cancer, and Dr. Berman is one of their top doctors. I'll give you her number so you can make an appointment."

I felt touched by Dr. Kopel's concern. He wanted us to make sure we felt comfortable with what he was doing. How many doctors urge their patients to go for second opinions?

As we left the office and started home, Mother said, "I suppose we ought to go consult this Dr. Berman, but I have every confidence in Dr. Kopel and the other doctors at Maimonides."

"So do I," said Reuven, "but it is always a good idea to get a second opinion. It pays to be as sure as you can be that you're doing the right thing."

When we got home, we called Dr. Ellen Berman. We managed to get an appointment for the following week.

"It's going to be some exciting week," I said to Reuven. "First the blood testing, and then Dr. Berman."

"You have strange ideas of what's exciting," Reuven told me with a grin.

A week later, Father drove Mother, Moshe, Eli and me to be tested at the blood bank in Manhattan. They would test the blood for Human Leukocyte Antigen, or HLA, to see if any of my family members had the same exact bone marrow type as I did.

"Are you nervous?" I asked Eli. He was only thirteen. This couldn't have been easy for him.

"I'm not too happy about the needle," he admitted. "But it's worth doing it for you. I just hope I'm your match!"

Mother and I exchanged glances over his head. The look of pride in her eyes didn't need to be put into words.

We arrived promptly for our appointment at the blood bank. We were escorted to comfortable recliners and told to sit down, and then the nurses gently drew two tubes of blood from each person's arm. When they came to me, they took six tubes, since they would need to do many additional tests on my blood.

"That wasn't too bad," Father said cheerfully as he drove us home.

"The hard part is waiting for an answer." Mother sighed. "It's going to be a long week."

A few days later, we drove to Sloan-Kettering in Manhattan for our consultation with Dr. Ellen Berman, an efficient, pleasant woman. She gave me a thorough check-up and a blood test before she studied my bone marrow slides. Then she and her assistant asked me many questions about my treatment, the chemo and the medications I had taken. Reuven supplied many of the details.

Finally, Dr. Berman said, "Well, Mrs. Panzer, it seems you've been receiving excellent treatment. If you had been here in Sloan-Kettering, the doctors would have followed the exact same protocol."

"You've really set my mind at ease," I said. "And what about the bone marrow transplant? What do you think we should do?"

Dr. Berman put her fingertips together and glanced down at her notes. "If, as Dr. Kopel told you, you have been diagnosed as having APL, I agree that a bone marrow transplant may not be necessary. You are young and otherwise healthy. If you were my patient, I would recommend that you be subjected to several rounds of high-dose chemotherapy before risking a transplant. Of course, it would be wise to discover now whether or not you have a match with a member of your family. An autologous transplant is always a possibility, but a match with a sibling is probably safer. Is there anything else you'd like to ask?"

"No, I think we've covered everything," I said as I rose from my chair. "Thank you very much, Dr. Berman."

She also stood and took my hand in hers. "Good luck and best wishes for a speedy recovery."

Reuven and I walked quietly through the hospital corridor until we reached the entrance. "Reuven," I said, "I'm glad I ended up in Maimonides. The doctors are super, and Dr. Berman herself said the treatment wouldn't have been any different here. In Maimonides, I'm right in the middle of the community, but here I would really feel out of it. Now, I feel that I'm not just a "statistic," but a real person. We did the right thing."

"I think so, too," Reuven answered quietly.

With the extra peace of mind Dr. Berman had given us, we were now free to resume worrying about whether or not the HLA testing would show I had a match. We lifted the receiver each time the phone rang, instead of letting the answering machine take care of it. We knew it would take a week, but we couldn't help expecting to hear an answer any minute. We all beseeched Hashem to send us a match in case a bone transplant proved necessary.

Finally, Mother couldn't take the suspense anymore. She called herself to find out the results.

"The doctors will be informed, ma'am," was the infuriatingly calm response.

"When will they know?"

"All I can tell you is that the department heads are having a meeting about Malia Panzer's blood."

"A meeting?" Mother asked, bewildered. "Why do they need a meeting about it? Does she have a match or not?"

"I'm sure you'll be told when they know, ma'am."

Mother hung up the phone in frustration. "I guess we just have to wait," she sighed.

Finally, the phone rang. It was the call we'd been waiting for. Mother listened for a few moments, then whispered, "*Baruch Hashem.*" She hung up and turned to us with shining eyes.

"Malia has a match." She smiled broadly. "His name is Moshe Greenberg."

What shouting and jumping up and down there was at the news! Surely, anyone who would have peeked in the windows at that moment would have thought we were insane. Cheering and dancing over bone marrow transplants? But we were so grateful to Hashem that a perfect sibling match was available. Hopefully, I wouldn't need it, but if I did, it was available.

Three weeks after I left the hospital, it was time to speak to Dr. Kopel again and decide how to attempt to get rid of the leukemia for good.

Dr. Kopel broke off his whistling as we entered the office. "Hello," he said. "You're looking good, Malia."

I smiled, but I wasn't so sure about that. Once I'd drained the excess fluids from my body through medication and walking, I lost all the extra weight—and I kept on losing. There had been too many days when I hadn't eaten, and even now, I had very little appetite. I was much too thin now. I weighed just over one hundred pounds.

"I've discussed your case with several other specialists," he told me. "After considering all the factors, we agree it would be best to try the high-dose chemo first. You're young and healthy; that's good. As for the transplant, it's best to avoid it if we can. The radiation can damage other organs in the body. And it would probably destroy your ability to have more children." He looked grave. "In addition, there is the danger of the host body rejecting the grafted bone marrow. There are far fewer risks with chemotherapy. If the chemo fails, we will reconsider the possibility of a transplant."

We talked a little more, but I wasn't listening too well. The dangers of a transplant sent chills up my spine, but I refused to think about it. I had to preserve my optimism and positive outlook. Why worry about the transplant if the doctor had just told me that I had a very good chance with chemotherapy? I thanked Hashem that I was young, strong and healthy, and I could be treated with high-dose chemotherapy. I knew it wouldn't be a picnic, but I was lightheaded with relief. Worry has to be constructive, something to help you deal with a difficult situation, to find the right solutions. Worrying about something that may never happen, however, is destructive. It eats away at your spirit and eventually your body as well. Right now, I was determined not to worry about the risks of a transplant. I was ready to be "zapped." Full speed ahead!

As we waited for the elevator, I turned to Mother and saw the worry lines etched into her forehead.

Impulsively, I hugged her and exclaimed, "I'm starting chemo!"

She looked startled for a moment, then a smile spread slowly across her face, smoothing away those awful worry lines. My optimism was too contagious to resist. "Yes, you're starting chemo!" she shouted back. "Hooray!"

The other people waiting for the elevator turned and stared at us. Who ever heard of two women excited by the idea of chemotherapy? They probably thought we were crazy. How could they understand our great joy that Hashem had granted us the opportunity for me to be cured of leukemia for good?

Consolidation Chemotherapy 12

That Friday, I was readmitted to Maimonides Hospital for my second round of chemo, called "consolidation." This time, the drugs would be much more powerful, so strong that they spread the six doses, each lasting four hours, over a five-day period.

I found myself back on my original floor in the Gellman building. I didn't need to be in isolation, as my numbers were still at safe levels.

As soon as I was settled, I went to peek into my old room. Rose was still there. I was a little saddened to know she was still in the hospital, but it was nice to see her friendly face.

"Hello, Malia," she said, smiling more with her eyes than her mouth. She looked tired.

"Hi," I said cheerfully. "Well, here I am again. They're giving me high dosages of chemo. Let's hope that does the trick!"

"Yes, let's hope," she said. She gazed at me in a strange way, then she nodded. "You'll be fine, Malia. I really believe that. You're so full of life, and you've got such a wonderful outlook. I wish I could say the same for myself."

"Don't say that, Rose," I protested. "You have to have faith in Hashem, no matter how hopeless your situation may seem to you. Nothing is beyond His power."

"Yeah, I know," she said wearily.

I didn't know what to tell her. Somehow, my protestations of faith seemed inadequate. I guess faith is something that has to be deep inside you, something that becomes part of your very being. Otherwise, even if you believe in Hashem, it is only an intellectual knowledge. It doesn't change the way you feel in your heart. I wished I could get Rose to connect with Hashem, to bring Him into her life in a meaningful way, but I didn't know what to say.

"Don't be so upset, Malia," she was saying. "I'm hanging on. I'm doing the best I can. But let's not talk about me. Let's talk about you. You've come to the right place if you want to know about dealing with chemo. You know it's going to be tough, don't you?"

"Yes, I do, Rose. I'm ready for it."

"Ice."

"Ice?"

"Crushed ice. That's one of the tricks you need to know. You're going to get very nauseous from all that stuff they're going to give you. Suck on crushed ice. It helps. Trust me."

For the next few minutes, Rose gave me the benefit of her experience with chemotherapy and how to deal with its side effects. Then one of the nurses shooed me out and pulled the curtain around her bed. I called out a quiet goodbye and left.

Before the chemo began, I was premedicated with the drugs that would hopefully counteract the side effects of the chemo. This time, because the dosage was so strong, I was also given eye drops to prevent conjunctivitis, as well as additional anti-nausea medication. The IV went in on Friday afternoon, and my second round of chemo began.

Shabbos came quietly. I received the second dose of chemo that morning. It took three or four hours for the drugs to drip through the IV in my arm.

"It was easier with the central line," Mother observed. "It's a little painful, isn't it?"

"Nothing I can't handle," I said cheerfully.

Later that day, a doctor came into the room, holding a consent form. "Hello, Malia," he said. "I'm here to tell you about the surgery you're getting tomorrow."

"Oh, am I getting surgery?"

"It wouldn't be wise to use a peripheral IV in your arm constantly during all these rounds of chemo and the transfusions afterwards," he explained. "Dr. Plantilla has you scheduled to undergo surgery for an infusaport tomorrow."

"Is that the same as a central line?" Mother asked. "That's what she had last time."

He shook his head. "The infusaport is better, because it's a long-term device. It can remain under the patient's skin for months, or even years, while a central line could cause infection if it's left inside indefinitely."

"How exactly does it work?" I was curious to know about this device I would apparently be carrying around with me for some time.

"The infusaport is similar to an IV that leads directly into the central vein in your chest. It's sewn in underneath the skin. Any needle inserted into your skin goes directly into the infusaport and from there into your central vein. No trouble with collapsed veins or infections. No need for constant replacements. And no constant pricks!"

"Sounds good to me," I said.

"Good. In that case, please sign this consent form." He handed me the sheet.

With an apologetic look, I handed it back. "I'm sorry," I said, "but I can't sign on Shabbos. It'll have to wait until after the stars come out tonight. If you leave it here, I'll sign it as soon as I can and give it to the nurses."

The doctor was taken aback, but he soon recovered. "Of course," he said. "I forgot. My apologies. Don't worry about it. I'll take it with me and bring it back tonight."

That night, I waited for the doctor to return. I suppose he did-
n't want to make the same mistake again, because he waited until
midnight before he brought the consent form. I couldn't really
read it, since the constant eye drops made my vision blurry, but I
signed it willingly and prepared myself for surgery in the morning.

The attendant was in my room with a stretcher at 7:30 in the
morning. It was nice to see Dr. Plantilla's cheerful face. He gave me
a local anaesthetic, so I was able to talk to him throughout the
surgery. I was finished by 9:00, when Dr. Plantilla called up to my
room to tell Mother and Reuven that the surgery had gone well and
I was in the recovery room. As they had done when they inserted
the central line, I was taken for X-rays to make sure my lungs
weren't damaged by the insertion of the infusaport. By 11:15, I was
back in my room on the next dose of ARA-C! I was still on the
peripheral IV, as the site of the infusaport had to heal before it could
be used.

The trouble began that evening. As usual when I was on chemo,
I had no appetite. I'd managed an Ensure high-calorie malted during the day, but at 7:00, I threw it up.

"I'm really not feeling well," I admitted to Reuven as he hovered
over me.

The nurse took my temperature. Sure enough, I was running
a fever.

"Maybe if I walk around a little, I'll feel better," I said hopefully.
But I began to feel chest pain, and it grew steadily worse.

Concerned, Mother called Dr. Bashevkin, one of the doctors on the
hematology/oncology team. He had given us his home phone number
long ago, as had the other doctors. She described the pains I was feeling. "And she says it's growing worse," Mother told him anxiously.

Dr. Bashevkin was silent for a moment. Then he asked, "Has
Malia vomited since the infusaport was put in?"

"Why, yes," Mother said, surprised. "How did you know?"

"Don't worry," Dr. Bashevkin said with a small sigh. "It will all
be taken care of in the morning."

Monday morning, at 9:00, I found myself back downstairs, getting ready for an X-ray. "But I just had one yesterday," I said, bewildered. "Why do I need one again now?"

"It's just to make sure there's nothing wrong with your lungs after the surgery," the technician explained after examining my file.

"But isn't that what yesterday's X-ray was for?"

"I'm not a doctor," he said with a shrug. "They ordered an X-ray for you, so I'm giving it."

I found out the answer all too soon. I had a pneumothorax—a hole in the lung!

Back in my room, Dr. Bashevkin explained how this had happened. "When the infusaport was put in, your left lung received a tiny nick," he told me. "It was so small that it didn't even show on the X-ray we took right after the surgery. Here, take a look." He showed me the picture that had been taken yesterday. Sure enough, the lungs looked perfectly clear.

"Ordinarily, a hole that small can easily heal on its own," he went on. "But when you vomited, the force propelled a lot of air out of your lungs and into your chest cavity. Now, the hole was widened, and you can't exhale properly. That's why you feel so much pain."

"So what do we do about it?" Reuven asked anxiously.

"We'll have to put in a chest tube for a few days to pull out the excess air and help Malia's lungs expand. It won't be pleasant," he said to me with a rueful smile, "but it will only be for a day. That should take care of it."

Dr. Bashevkin ordered a Duragesic patch #25 for me. This is a kind of painkiller applied directly to the skin, where it is absorbed into the bloodstream. To me, it looked like nothing more than an extra-wide piece of Scotch tape, but it did alleviate the pain. I was still hurting quite a bit, and I didn't want to think about how much pain I would be feeling without it.

Just before noon, Dr. Plantilla came up to my room. This time, he inserted a blue tube through a small hole he made in the left side of my chest. The tube was connected to a small, water-filled box lying on the floor. The excess air would then escape through the tube into the box, which bubbled to show that air was coming in.

The moment the tube was in, we all heard a lot of noise. "Good," Dr. Plantilla said with satisfaction. He pointed at the box, which was bubbling wildly. "A lot of air came out right away. That's a good sign."

"Does that mean she doesn't have to have the tube in for so long?" Reuven asked hopefully.

"I'm afraid not," Dr. Plantilla replied. "Malia will still need the chest tube for at least twenty-four hours, if not more. Her lungs must expand fully." He rose and connected the water-filled box to a port in the wall. "I'm going to connect the suction. That will make the air come out faster." He looked down at me. "Good luck," he added quietly.

This was the hardest thing I had gone through yet during the entire ordeal. During the induction phase, when I first came to the hospital after Pesach, stopping to nurse "cold turkey" had been the hardest thing. But this was much more painful, even worse than labor pains. Every breath was agony. I was afraid to inhale too deeply. What if I caused further damage to my lungs? The doctors assured me I couldn't do any harm, but I still concentrated on breathing shallowly, trying to ignore the terrible pain.

That same afternoon, still attached to the chest tube, I was taken downstairs for another X-ray. My bubbling box rode piggyback on the back of my wheelchair. I was still hurting badly.

The following day, Tuesday, was day number five for my chemotherapy—the last day. The whole chest tube area seemed to radiate pain. Dr. Bashevkin ordered me another medicine patch, this one of greater strength. It helped a little, but every breath still hurt.

That night, trying to fall asleep, I found it impossible to find a comfortable position. Mother watched me twist and turn gingerly, hampered by the IV in one arm, the chest tube on my left side, the soreness of the infusaport site that had not finished healing and my general weakness. I could barely move.

With her help, I finally managed to roll onto my stomach, where I hoped I would be more comfortable. My right hand caught underneath me, and I simply could not pull it out or get up. Mother helped me into a sitting position, and I stayed that way the entire night.

Mother dozed off in the recliner chair. I remained sitting up, slightly hunched over, still trying not to breathe too deeply. At about 4:00 in the morning, Mother opened her eyes and saw I was still awake.

"Is there anything I can do?" she offered.

I gave her a weak smile. "Maybe, if you wouldn't mind, we could play a game or something. Anything to help the time pass. I just want this night to end already!"

Bubbi Rothman had long ago given me Skip-Bo and Rummy-Q to keep me occupied during my hospital stay. We turned on the light and played games for two hours. At 6:00, feeling utterly exhausted, I tried to go to sleep, but without success.

As Wednesday morning wore on, I kept watching the door. Every time someone came in, or even if I heard footsteps approaching in the hallway, I looked up, hoping to see Dr. Plantilla arriving to take out the chest tube. At last, he came into the room, having squeezed in time between surgeries.

"I'm so glad to see you!" I exclaimed.

He chuckled. "I'm glad you're excited to see me," he said.

"I'm excited to get this chest tube removed!"

With the chest tube out, I finally felt it was safe to take a good, deep breath. I would be able to go home that afternoon and start getting my strength back.

Dr. Kopel came by to check on me right after lunch. "I think we'll let you go home this afternoon," he told me. "Take it easy for the next few weeks. This is your time to regain your strength. Starting next week, you'll be getting transfusions and platelets as an outpatient. I'm also going to put you on Cipro, which is an antibiotic to prevent infection. Don't forget, your numbers are going to drop."

"When will we be able to start the next round of chemo?" I asked. The faster we did it, the sooner I'd be done!

"You're in a hurry, aren't you?" said Dr. Kopel. "Actually, there's some good news. There's a new medication called Neupogen that brings up your white count faster than it would rise on its own. If you take a daily shot of Neupogen, we'll be able to start your next round of chemo a week earlier."

"Will I get the shots in the hospital?"

"No, that's not necessary." Dr. Kopel looked at Mother. "Your mother can give them to you easily enough."

"Me?" Mother looked doubtful. "I've never given a shot before."

As an EMT, she had taken blood samples, stitched up the knee of a four-year-old who'd fallen on broken glass, saved children from choking and even delivered a baby, but giving shots was something new.

"I'll have one of the nurses show you how. Don't worry, it's quite simple. Take Malia home and bring her back to my office tomorrow afternoon for a checkup." He looked back at me. "Take care of yourself, Malia. I'll see you tomorrow."

Soon after Dr. Kopel left, my nurse, Marcia Gellis, came into the room. "So, Mrs. Greenberg," she said cheerfully. "You want to learn how to give shots?"

"That's right," said Mother.

Marcia handed Mother the needle. "You insert the needle subcutaneously, that means underneath the skin and into the tissue. Then you press the plunger. Like so." She demonstrated. "Now, you don't want to learn how on Malia, so you should practice first."

"On what?" Mother asked. "Thin air? That won't teach me anything. Do you know where I can get volunteers?"

"No, the only volunteers you'll find are in your refrigerator."

"My refrigerator?"

"That's right. Do you have any grapefruit at home?"

"Grapefruit?" Mother and I repeated simultaneously, feeling a little ridiculous to be echoing everything she said.

"Yes. Practice on a grapefruit. I know it sounds ridiculous, but the skin of the grapefruit will give you the same amount of resistance and the same feel as Malia's skin. Practice, Mrs. Greenberg. Malia doesn't get her first shot until tomorrow. Dr. Kopel said to tell you that he'll give you the Neupogen when you come into his office."

As soon as Reuven came back, Mother and I packed everything up and we went back home. Mother went straight into the kitchen and raided the fruit bin. I spent the evening curled up on the couch, dozing from time to time and watching with amusement as Mother practiced her shots over and over again on the poor grapefruit. Who would have thought to see a grown woman repeatedly stabbing a grapefruit with a syringe?

"Sometimes," I told Reuven, "it's easy to see the lighter side of things."

Reuven smiled. "Malia, you always will."

Precious Days

The following afternoon, Thursday, we went to Dr. Kopel's office for a checkup. After he examined me, he watched Mother give me the first shot of Neupogen.

"That's fine, Mrs. Greenberg," he said. "Don't worry about hurting Malia. A subcutaneous shot, pushed in at a ninety-degree angle, causes no pain. Here, look."

He took the needle, pushed up his sleeve, and gave himself a shot. The two of us stared at him with disbelief.

"You see?" he said. "It doesn't hurt." He put the needle down. "Malia, have you started the Cipro?"

"Yes," I answered.

"Good. Rest up over the weekend. Monday morning, you should be in K-8 at 8:30. Dr. Plantilla will check the infusaport to make sure it's healed before you begin your transfusions." He gave Mother the supply of Neupogen. "Keep up the shots. The faster and closer we make the rounds of chemo, the better it will be. Good luck!"

As soon as we got back home, I fell straight into bed. I was so exhausted I could barely see straight. For the rest of that day and most of Friday, I basically slept, waking only when Reuven brought me my meals. Late Friday afternoon, though, I was wide awake and tingling with anticipation. Rachel, who was back from Israel, bustled about the kitchen together with Mother. Reuven had gone to Monsey to pick up Dov, so we could spend Shabbos together. I was still pretty weak, so we decided to leave Ari in Monsey with my in-laws. One child at a time was all I could handle.

How wonderful to be with my son again! It was wonderful, too, to see him happy and positively blooming.

I barely rested that Shabbos. I spent every available moment playing with my precious son. We played games and read stories. I listened to Dov's happy babbling and felt I would burst with happiness. When Reuven drove him back to Monsey after Shabbos, I was on the verge of collapse, but it had been worth it.

Sunday, I once again spent most of the day asleep. Mother gave me another shot of Neupogen. She was quite proficient at it now.

Having Rachel home gave a real lift to my spirits, and they certainly needed a lift. We talked about my illness, my fears, my hopes, my constant and often difficult battle to remain totally positive in my outlook. We also talked about her wedding day, which was fast approaching. I felt guilty that everyone was making such a fuss over me at a time when she, the glowing bride, should have been the center of attention. But she was very sweet about it.

As she talked about all her plans, I couldn't help thinking about how strange life was. Just a few years earlier, I had been exactly where she was, just getting married, starry-eyed, full of excitement, on the threshold of a rosy, fairy-tale existence. How could I have known that just a few years later I would be fighting for my life against a dreaded disease? But that is all part of the wonder of life. You have to capture every moment and savor it to the fullest. You can't worry about the future, because that would ruin the present. There are no guarantees in life. No one knows what the future will bring, who will fall ill or be hit by a car, or anything else that might happen. All we can do is have faith in Hashem and live each day for itself. I truly believed that every day was precious, even days of terrible suffering such as I was enduring.

After all, hadn't this been a wonderful day? I asked myself. I had held my darling little boy in my arms and I had shared confidences with my beloved sister. Tomorrow I would forget the suffering, but I would treasure these memories forever.

The following morning, Reuven drove me to the hospital. Mother was teaching, but she planned to come to the hospital afterwards to take me home in the afternoon.

Before going up the eighth floor in the Kronish Building, we stopped at Dr. Plantilla's office. He checked the infusaport site as well as the chest tube site and gave me a nod of approval.

"This has healed just fine, Malia," he told me. "You've developed a bit of a scar over the infusaport site, but that is pretty common for someone with fair skin like yours. We'll take care of it when we take the infusaport out. G-d willing, that will be in the near future."

After I'd received Dr. Plantilla's stamp of approval, I went to K-8. It seemed strange to be in the hospital as an outpatient. The nurses were all friendly, so I was able to relax. A nurse named Geula had a baby the same age as Ari and we compared notes about the adventures of child rearing. Thanks to the infusaport, which I was now using for the first time, the transfusions were painless. It may be hard to believe, but we actually had a good time!

I was given a comfortable recliner. Once I was settled and relaxed, the nurses drew two tubes of blood. The first was discarded, in case it had come in contact with any germs; the second tube was sent across the street to the laboratory of Special Hematology for a complete blood count. On the days when Mother was able to be with me in the morning, she often volunteered to take it across for them. From the results of the CBC, they could determine exactly how much blood and platelets I needed for the day. Sometimes I only needed one or the other; sometimes I needed both.

By the time we got the results of the CBC, Mother had joined me in the hospital. My nurse that first day was Ellen Mitchell, a real comedian. She spent the morning cracking jokes and putting me at ease.

"Let's see," Ellen said as she read the report. "According to your blood results, you'll need two units of blood and one of platelets. How about your Neupogen shot? Have you had that today?"

"No. Mother hasn't given it to me yet."

"Well, let's watch." She stood there with her hands on her hips expectantly. "Mrs. Greenberg, please do the honors. I always enjoy watching someone else give the shot."

Mother filled the plunger expertly and inserted the needle carefully at ninety degrees. It was painless.

"I see you're an expert!" Ellen complimented. "A real pro!"

"Thanks," Mother said. She made a mock bow.

The rest of the day passed mostly in a soporific haze. Before I received a transfusion of blood, I was premedicated with Benedryl, hydrocortisone and Tylenol. The Benedryl usually put me to sleep. When I received platelets, I was premedicated with Demerol. This put me on a "high" and usually sent me off to dreamland, too. In fact, I used to look forward to getting transfusions of platelets, just so I could get the Demerol. As I joked to Reuven, "Now I can understand drug addicts!"

The nurses joked about it and simply woke me up for lunch, blood pressure checks and temperature checks. Dr. Kopel, who often came by to see how I was doing, often greeted me with, "Good morning, Sleeping Beauty!" Whenever I was awake and relatively alert, I jotted down various thoughts and notes in preparation for the book I had already decided to write.

By Thursday, my numbers were already beginning to rise. The transfusions and the Neupogen were doing the trick.

"Okay, you're free for now," Ellen told me. "Come back on Monday for another CBC and we'll see if you need any more transfusions."

I had another wonderful Shabbos with Reuven and Dov. I was glad to see I had much more strength than I'd had the previous week.

Early Monday morning, we went back for another blood prick. Dr. Kopel came into the room himself with the results. As usual, he was whistling happily.

"Your numbers are excellent, Malia," he told me, beaming. "We'll be able to start your next round of chemo this week. Go home. Enjoy the week. We'll see you back here on Friday."

Reuven, Mother and I practically floated out of the building on a cloud of joy.

"Let's go visit Bubbi," I suggested. "It'll be a nice surprise." I was in such high spirits that I wanted to share it with someone.

We got bagels and other breakfast foods and went to Bubbi Rothman's house. She was delighted to see us. We all enjoyed breakfast together, lingering over the table and talking happily.

Afterwards, Mother went off to school, and here we were, Reuven and I, alone together in the beautiful sunshine, no doctors to visit, no hospitals, no treatments. For the first time in a long while, we could enjoy the exquisite pleasures of a normal day of normal living.

"Let's go do something fun," Reuven suggested. "Where would you like to go? How about the Great Adventure amusement park?"

"I have a better idea," I said. "Let's go to Monsey and see the kids!"

Reuven and I drove straight to Monsey. Dov was at my sister-in-law's house, but Ari was there. I hugged him tightly and kissed him. I hadn't seen my precious baby since I'd gone into the hospital for consolidation. It seemed like months and months, even though it was only three weeks.

Within the hour, my sister-in-law drove up with Dov. As soon as he saw me, he ran straight across the driveway into my arms. He gave me a big hug and kiss, which I gave right back. It was hard to decide which of us was happier.

We spent the entire day in Monsey with our little boys. My mother-in-law wouldn't let me do anything except sit in the sun and enjoy the children. It was a truly marvelous day, but I couldn't wait to be with my children full-time.

A Time to Celebrate

14

My third round of chemotherapy began. By now, we had developed a routine. We were all packed and ready to go on Friday morning, awaiting the call from the hospital that would tell us my bed was free. Once we arrived, Mother helped me unpack before she went off to arrange for our little refrigerator and the recliner she used as a bed. Marcia Gellis, my wonderful nurse, had ordered an "egg crate" for my bed,[1] knowing I found it much more comfortable. She also called the "IV nurse" to come and access my infusaport, so I could get started on chemo right away. The sooner we started, the sooner we could leave.

This time, I was so absorbed by developments in the family that I barely noticed the side effects of the ARA-C as it dripped into my system. Moshe had been seeing a wonderful girl, and things were getting serious. The excitement mounted with each successive date. On Shabbos, Mother and I could not stop talking about Moshe's upcoming date on Sunday afternoon. When Father walked in from Flatbush and sang *zemiros* with us, that was all we could talk about. What would tomorrow bring?

---

1. A pad with bumps and indentations similar to the cardboard trays used for eggs. This eliminates pressure on the body of a bedridden patient.

Sunday arrived dark and overcast. I didn't care. I didn't care about my lack of appetite, either. All I cared was that Moshe had left the house for his date at 4:00 in the afternoon. Everyone in the family was waiting with bated breath, waiting to hear the good news.

The afternoon had never passed so slowly. Early that morning, the chemo had taken the usual four hours to drip in at 166 drips an hour. Usually, I slept while Mother counted every drip, but today, I was so keyed up by anticipation that even the medication couldn't make me doze off. Now, as the afternoon wore on, I found myself more awake than ever. I kept fidgeting, staring at the silent phone. Why didn't it ring already? When would we hear what was happening?

The skies cracked open as night fell. It was pouring heavily, a real thunderstorm complete with great jagged flashes of lightning. We still hadn't heard from Moshe.

At midnight, Mother's beeper finally went off. She snatched it off the little table. Sure enough, Father had called. She called back quickly, listened for a moment and practically jumped into the air. "It's official!" Mother yelled, forgetting for the moment that we were in the hospital. "Moshe is engaged!"

She bent over to hug me, then she frowned. "We've got a little problem here. The young couple just walked into our house, and her parents are coming over. I expected this to happen much earlier, and that Reuven would be able to cover for me while I went to the house for a *lechaim*. But now it's late, and they won't let Reuven in to stay with you. I don't know what to do."

"I could stay by myself for a little while," I offered.

"Out of the question," Mother said. "You'll be starting your next dose of chemo soon. This is no time for you to be alone." She stood up. "Let me talk to the head nurse. Maybe we can work something out."

She was back in a few minutes, looking happy.

"It's all taken care of. I explained the situation, and they were very understanding. They said Reuven can't stay overnight, since that's hospital policy, but it will be okay for him to come for a few hours. As soon as he comes, I'll run over to the house and then come right back."

Within half an hour, Father and Reuven were in the room, their faces shining with joy. I wished Father a big *mazel tov* and told Mother she should take her time. Father left with Mother. Reuven sat down next to my bed, and we spent the next half-hour talking excitedly. Then, worn out from the suspenseful waiting and drugged by all the medication, I fell asleep.

When I awoke early the next morning, I found Mother dozing in her recliner. She seemed to sense my movement and sat up.

"Oh, Malia!" she exclaimed. "It was so beautiful! Ruthie is such a sweetie. I know you'll love her. We had the most wonderful time. The only thing missing was you! I took a video, though, so I'll pop it into the VCR whenever you're ready to see it. I taped the entire thing, from beginning to end."

"That's wonderful," I said. Then I rubbed my blurry eyes. "I can't wait to see the video, but I don't think I'll be able to watch it until I've finished with the chemo and I'm off the eye drops. I'll have a chance to see it pretty soon."

"The engagement party is on Thursday night," Mother told me. "You'll be out of the hospital by then. I hope you'll be there."

Father, however, looked doubtful. "But what about germs? Won't it be dangerous?"

"I'll ask Dr. Kopel," I promised.

At about 10:00 that morning, the phone rang. Reuven picked it up, listened for a moment, then handed me the receiver. "It's Moshe," he announced.

I grabbed the phone. "Moshe? *Mazel tov*! You can't believe how excited I am! I can't wait to meet Ruthie. Wow, you and Rachel both engaged at the same time!"

I was talking so fast that it took a minute or two before Moshe even had a chance to say anything. "Listen, Malia. I want to bring Ruthie over to the hospital to meet you. Is it okay?"

I was longing to see her, but I had to be honest with myself and with Moshe. "This morning isn't really the best. I'm not feeling that great, and I don't think I'm up to company right now. But will you please call later? Maybe I'll feel better in the afternoon."

Sure enough, by 2:00 in the afternoon, I was more than ready for company. I called Moshe and he promised to be there within a few hours.

I was so excited, I felt I had to share the good news with someone else. The nurses all knew about it already. Whom could I tell? Rose! Together with Mother, I took the short walk to her room. She was lying quietly in bed, but she propped herself up to a sitting position when I came in. I hurried over to her bed and told her what had happened.

"Is that the one with the big glasses and the big smile?" Rose asked. She chuckled. "Hey, you know something? That describes all your brothers!"

"They're coming to visit me in a little while," I told her happily. "Should I bring them in to say hello?"

"I'm afraid that's out of the question," a nurse said from behind me. "Sorry, Malia. Back to your room now. This excitement isn't good for Rose."

I obediently got to my feet. "I'll tell you about it later," I promised as I headed for the door. "See you!"

I went back to my room and climbed back into bed. Even that little excursion down the hall and back had tired me out.

As Ruthie told me later, she felt quite nervous as she and Moshe drove together to Maimonides Hospital. This was their first outing after being officially engaged, and they were going to a hospital to visit a sister undergoing chemotherapy for leukemia. She had no idea of my condition, but she pictured a wan, sickly girl lying in a hospital bed, able to speak only in a faint whisper. As they rode the elevator up to the eighth floor of the Gellman building, Ruthie prepared herself for the worst.

As they passed the nurses' desk, they were greeted with friendly smiles. "Congratulations! We heard you're engaged. Malia is so happy. We're happy for you, too!" Ruthie felt a little dazed by all this.

As soon as they entered the room, I jumped out of bed, shouting at Mother, "Oh, wow! They're here!" I ran straight for Ruthie and hugged her tightly. "I'm so excited to finally meet you. I've heard so much about you. Welcome to the family!"

They were there only for a little while, being thoughtful enough not to overstay their welcome and tire me out. Still, in that short time, Ruthie and I hit it off right away. I felt as if she were already my sister. With such joy in the family, how could I not feel like I was flying?

Dr. Kopel visited me later that evening. I told him our exciting news. "I already heard," he told me, whistling a bar or two of wedding music. "Congratulations."

"Will I be able to go to the engagement party?" I asked hopefully. "It's on Thursday night."

Dr. Kopel considered for a moment. "That's only seven days after you began the chemo. Your numbers won't have dropped yet. You'll already be on the Cipro and the Neupogen." He thought for a few moments, then he nodded. "I see no reason why you can't go if you're feeling up to it. Be sensible, of course. Take it easy, don't overexert yourself, and you'll be fine."

The following morning, I received my sixth and final dose of chemo for round three. Reuven helped me pack and prepare to leave.

"There's a lot to do," I warned him. "I'm going to have to find a new outfit." I was still very underweight. None of my things fit me properly. Since I spent much of my time dressed in a robe, I hadn't really worried about it before, but I would certainly need to buy something now!

As it turned out, I found a new outfit pretty quickly. It was a good thing, too, because I still hadn't recovered from the chemo.

The first place we visited was one of the most popular dress stores in Flatbush. It was a good choice, because it had an excellent selection of styles and sizes, but it was also very noisy and crowded, not exactly what I needed in my condition.

Mother and I found a rack of dressy outfits, but I didn't have the strength to look through the garments and make a selection. I needed to lean against a wall for a while to catch my breath, but there were no bare walls in sight. Every inch of wall space was covered by either a rack of garments or some other kind of merchandise display. Finally, I found an unoccupied mirror and leaned against it. Just in time.

"You just stay here, Malia," Mother said. "I'll look for things and bring them to you for approval. Just try and take it easy."

I nodded and closed my eyes. My head was swimming. It was also hot in the store, and I felt a sheen of perspiration gathering on my forehead. Hang on for a little while, I told myself. Just a few minutes and we'll be out of here.

But it took more than a few minutes, and in truth, how could I realistically have expected to be out of there in a few minutes? Nothing ever takes a few minutes, especially not shopping for a fancy dress.

A little while later, Mother came over to me with an armful of dresses.

"What do you think of these, Malia?" she said as she held them up for my inspection. "I think this one would bring out the color of your eyes, don't you agree?'

The color of my eyes was the furthest thing from mind right then. I tried to get involved in the process of choosing a dress, but they all looked like blotches of color to me. I was feeling increasingly woozy. I felt my knees buckling.

"Mother, I have to sit down," I whispered. "I can't stand another minute."

She glanced at me sharply, her eyes wide with sudden alarm. She flung the dress over a rack and ran off to find me a chair. Moments later, she returned with a stepladder stool.

"Here, Malia," she said. "Sit on this and lean against the mirror while I go find you a real chair."

From behind Mother, we heard a throat clear. We both looked up and saw a saleslady looking at us with keen interest. She had a tape measure draped around her neck.

"Pardon me," she said, "but is everything all right?"

"Everything is just fine," Mother reassured her. "We're looking for a dress for her brother's wedding. My daughter is just feeling a little faint."

The saleslady nodded knowingly. "Of course. I understand. Expecting a little visitor, are we?"

I blushed, but I had no strength to respond. Mother did, however. "Well, not exactly, ma'am. Not exactly."

"Oh," said the saleslady, suddenly flustered. "I'm so sorry. I didn't mean . . . Is everything all right? Can I bring you a glass of water, young lady? Should I call for some help, maybe?"

"No, I'm just fine," I said. I leaned back and felt the mirror press up against my spine. "If you want to help, you could bring me a chair."

She disappeared as mysteriously as she had appeared, and she returned a minute later with a nice padded chair. She must have gotten it from the office. It was heaven-sent.

"You just sit here, young lady," she told me, "I'll find you a nice dress. I have just the perfect dress in mind, and we carry it in all sizes."

"My daughter is usually a size 8," Mother said to her. "She lost some weight, so I think we should try a size 6, all right?"

The saleslady gave me an appraising look. "Yes, I see. She does look a little gaunt. We'll try a size 6, but that might also be just a little large."

She was right on both counts. As she had said, the dress was really perfect, pretty, feminine and very festive without being overdone. And as she had warned us, the size 6 turned out to be more than a little large, but it took me a long time to find that out. There were a few times when I thought I would faint in the dressing room. I was like a robot going through the motions of putting on the dress without being fully aware of where I was and what I was doing. Finally, I got the dress on, just a little bit askew, and I went out to show it to Mother.

"Malia, the dress is swimming on you!" she exclaimed.

The saleslady smiled with satisfaction, but she said nothing.
"Perhaps we should try a size 4," Mother suggested to her.
"Yes, I would say so," she said.

As it turned out the size 4 was also too large on me. I was so thin that I needed a size 2. It was incredible!

Thursday morning, I began to feel apprehensive about the engagement party. I hadn't really been seen in public since I had gone into the hospital right after Pesach. I knew how I looked. I was pale and thin, with no eyebrows or eyelashes. Would everyone stare at me? Would everyone be overly sympathetic? I didn't want people to feel sorry for me. Everything was going so well. How would I handle this?

At lunchtime, Father again voiced his concern. "Are you sure you want to do this?" he asked. "I'm worried about all the germs."

"Dr. Kopel said it was okay," I replied staunchly. "I do want to be there, really. I'll be all right."

We arrived at the hall about half an hour before the festivities were scheduled to begin. My head was already thumping from nervousness and exhaustion. We'd had supper just before I came, and I'd eaten my first whole meal in weeks. I felt sick. I looked at the arrangements and the flowers and had a sudden attack of nerves. I wanted to go home.

With a quiet word to Mother, I went into the bathroom and locked myself in. I sat down and put my head in my hands. I couldn't help wondering if I had made a big mistake by coming here. What was I doing here making believe I was a regular person? Why was I pretending that I could do normal things, the sort that other people did? Right now, I was very far from a normal person. I was very sick, fighting desperately for my life, and what was the point of making believe otherwise? I would have been much better off staying home, resting, sleeping, doing anything else but sitting in some strange bathroom feeling sorry for myself.

I felt a wave of nausea sweep over me, and I gasped for breath. Fortunately, it passed as quickly as it had come.

I thought about the comb of my wig. Ordinarily, it would lodge tightly in my hair so that my wig remained firmly in place. Now, however, the comb just scraped on my bald head, securing nothing. And it hurt!

Another wave of nausea swept over me, but this time there was no escape. I threw up everything I had eaten.

I washed my mouth and took off my wig. Then I just sat there without thinking or doing anything at all, just a blank young woman in a cramped little bathroom trying to get a grip on herself. After half an hour, I felt better and more prepared to face the world. I fixed myself up and went outside.

The party had already begun, and it was easy to let myself get caught up in the excitement. I soon found myself talking excitedly, forgetting my missing eyelashes and eyebrows and simply enjoying myself. After a few minutes, I found myself a chair and sat down in a corner. Dr. Kopel had said there wasn't really any need to worry about germs, but I wanted to be sure. Besides, I knew it would make Father feel better. Enough people came up to talk to me that I didn't feel left out at all.

About an hour later, Reuven came in with Dov. We'd decided to bring Dov back from Monsey that night instead of the following afternoon. Dov was very excited; he was staying up late and he got to be with Mommy! I spent the rest of the night sitting in my corner, holding my precious son and enjoying myself immensely. It was truly a beautiful celebration. As for myself, how could I complain? I was alive, even if not exactly well, and I was together with the people I loved. It was truly a time to celebrate. I prayed silently to Hashem that I would have many more occasions to celebrate in the future.

Happy Birthday 15

My Hebrew birthday, the 23rd of Tammuz, was on the Monday of my fourth round of chemotherapy. Even the sunshine peeking through the little window seemed brighter that morning. Clogged ears, blurred vision and loss of appetite couldn't mask the cheerful feeling of having reached my 23rd birthday. Traditionally, Jewish people wish each other long life "until one hundred and twenty years." According to my math, that gave me another ninety-seven to go.

Reuven came in that morning holding a huge bouquet of helium balloons. We tied them to the crank on the foot of my bed, where they bobbed and nodded at me. Many people called with birthday wishes: Gavriel and David from Israel, my in-laws and Dov from Monsey. Bubbi Rothman came to visit me, of course, and so did Moshe and Ruthie. It was a special day, and it seemed that all the chemo was dripping into my system more quickly than ever.

My last dose of chemo for this round was at 3:00 in the morning. By 9:00 Tuesday morning, when Dr. Ruben stopped in my room, I was dressed and packed, ready to leave as soon as I would be discharged.

"You're not happy to leave us, are you, Malia?" he said in mock surprise.

"I sure am!" I answered firmly.

Before I left, I peeked in on Rose. She was very weak and thin; she couldn't eat, and they had put her on a liquid diet. Her doctors were considering surgery. I told her I would say *Tehillim* for her and wished her a speedy recovery.

Now that I was out of the hospital, I had until Sunday to enjoy myself before my numbers dropped and I would need blood and platelets. With such a good round of chemo behind me, I was determined to make the most of these few days and do whatever I could.

Once again, I found myself thinking about how I had begun to view my life as a string of individual days, each precious and irreplaceable in its own right. With the specter of leukemia hanging over my head, each day was a victory, each good day an experience of the most incredible sweetness. I thought of all the people who lived normal lives, who gobbled up day after wonderful day without savoring each one or appreciating the sheer delight of living, without thanking the Master of the Universe with all their hearts for the gift of life. I believed deep in my heart that I would beat this disease and survive. Hashem had been kind to me, and I was making great progress. One day, I would join those people living normal lives, but I resolved that never would I take a single minute of existence for granted, never again would I cease to thank Him for the blessing of life.

Wednesday morning, Mother and Rachel addressed invitations for the wedding at the dining room table. I was allowed to sit there and join the conversation. Anything more, Mother insisted, would be too strenuous. But in my state of mind, just sitting there idle but content was such a thrilling experience. I could not believe that skydivers leaping out of airplanes experienced a greater thrill.

Soon after we finished, my Aunt Shani came by. We exchanged some playful banter before we went into the kitchen to bake *challah*.

Aunt Shani and Mother braided the dough. They were kind enough to allow me to stick in the raisins. After that, we whipped up some apple *kugels* and saw them safely into the oven. I felt so happy being in a domestic setting, even though I wasn't really doing anything to help.

"Great," Mother said as the last *kugel* was taken out of the oven and the *challos* were cooling on the counter. "What should we do now?"

"Let's go out for lunch," Shani proposed. She looked at me. "That'll be all right, won't it?"

"There's no reason not to," I said. "My numbers haven't dropped. I'm not even on Neupogen and Cipro yet."

We invited Rachel to come along, but she declined, saying it was my special treat. So Mother, Shani and I went to Weiss's Restaurant on Coney Island Avenue for lunch. We had a super time, and incredibly, I had enough appetite to eat a real meal for a change.

When it was time to leave, we discovered that the sky had clouded over and it was raining heavily outside.

"Oops," Mother muttered to herself as she peered out into a sea of raindrops. "What do we do now?"

"Malia can't walk home through this," Shani agreed. "She might catch cold, Heaven forbid."

"Maybe Father could pick us up?" I suggested. "If he's home, that is."

Mother went to the back of the restaurant to use the phone, but there was no answer. "Rachel must have gone out, too," she sighed. "Any other ideas?" She snapped her fingers and answered herself. "The car service at the corner! I'll be right back."

She was back within minutes, but without a car. "There's nothing available."

"Tell you what," Shani said. "My sister-in-law lives two blocks away. We can go there and get a ride home the rest of the way."

So we hurried through the rain as fast as we could for the two short blocks to Shani's sister-in-law. We were greeted warmly and treated to a comfortable ride home, safe and dry.

The following day, buoyed by my little adventure and still feeling strong enough to accomplish something, I went downstairs to Mother's basement. There, for the first time, I saw the incredible clutter of all the things Reuven had taken from our apartment by himself. While we'd been living in a furnished apartment, we did have tons of stuff: clothing, pots and dishes, kitchen appliances, baking pans and mixing bowls, silverware, glasses, serving trays, linens and tablecloths, boxes and boxes of *sefarim*, toys, the baby swing, the crib, the playpen and much, much more.

For a few minutes, I just stood there in awe, amazed at the amount of sheer energy it must have taken for Reuven to accomplish such a move on his own. Then, rolling up my sleeves, I set to work.

Mother wasn't so sure I should be doing things like this, but I was enjoying myself so much she decided not to argue and simply joined me. The two of us worked cheerfully through the day. By the time Mother had to go upstairs to get supper ready, all our things were packed neatly into boxes in the storage room. Mother's downstairs bedrooms were once again available for guests.

My in-laws were planning to be away that Shabbos, and they brought both children to stay with us. They would be back on Monday. I loved every minute I spent with my precious boys, but by Sunday morning, I was worn out. Much as I enjoyed it, playing with them took a lot out of me. The children were getting restless, and Mother and I decided to take them to the Brooklyn Children's Museum. We had a marvelous time and capped the outing by having pizza and ice cream for lunch. But as we walked out of the store and started down the avenue, I suddenly stopped.

"What is it?" Mother asked with concern.

I closed my eyes. "I feel dizzy," I said softly. "Faint."

We walked into the nearest store, and I sat down. Mother went off to use the phone, and in less than ten minutes, Father arrived to drive us home.

Mother gave me a drink and sent me straight to bed. I was fast asleep within minutes. Some time later, I awoke to the sight of Reuven's anxious eyes looking at me. Calmly, I reassured him that I was fine. True, I'd really overdone it. But it was worth it. I had such a fantastic time.

The following morning, Mother took me to K-8 for my transfusions. I greeted my nurses warmly, and Geula and I exchanged notes about our babies, as usual. Then I settled onto my comfortable lounge chair and got ready for a day of blood and platelets transfusions.

Wednesday afternoon, Mother discovered that the person who had gone to donate platelets for me for the following day had been anemic, and we were unable to find a replacement on such short notice. Mother came into K-8, where I was still receiving a transfusion, to tell me what was happening.

"I guess you won't be able to get platelets tomorrow," she said with a sigh. "Let's hope you won't need it. It could be a problem."

Dr. Bashevkin, overhearing Mother's comment, raised his eyebrows. "Not necessarily," he said. "It's true that a leukemic patient needs to have six to eight units of platelets from one person, but that person doesn't have to be someone who specifically donated it for Malia. I'm sure we can get undirected platelets if we have to."

I was slightly awed by the thought. Unlike donating blood, which is a relatively simple procedure, donating platelets involves being hooked up for a full ninety minutes with a needle in both arms. I'd been overwhelmed by the generous outpouring of kindness by those who had donated their blood and platelets for me, but the thought of someone simply walking into the Greater Blood Bank in Manhattan and donating platelets for anyone who might need it was incredibly inspiring.

Thank you, whoever you are, I thought the following day as I received a transfusion of undirected single-donor platelets. Thank you for caring about someone you'll never know.

Thursday night came with a terrible headache. Reuven was alarmed, but I was sure it was caused by an incoming wisdom tooth. Nonetheless, Reuven insisted I tell Dr. Bashevkin about the headache when we met the next morning in K-8, where I was scheduled for a blood count.

Dr. Bashevkin listened to my description of the headache, then said, "You know, Malia, your husband is right. It's critical that we know exactly what you're feeling so we can deal with problems as soon as they come up."

"It's just a headache," I said. "Why make such a big deal about it?"

"Because it could be a sign of something serious," he pointed out. "In your case, a headache could mean internal bleeding, Heaven forbid. Now that we know about your headache, we're going to try and find out why."

"Okay," I acquiesced. "What do we do?"

"First we've got to get a manual blood count to make sure your numbers are still up. That will rule out internal bleeding."

A short while later, we had the results. My numbers were just fine. "Okay," I told Dr. Bashevkin, "what now?"

"Now we look further. We're going to take a good look at your eyes."

He led me into a side room that had equipment for checking the eye. The bright spot of light aimed directly at my pupil made my eyes water, but I made the effort to keep them open. After a moment, Dr. Bashevkin sat back, frowning.

"What's wrong?" I asked. Icy fingers of terror gripped at my heart.

"I can't see the entire disc of your eye."

"What does that mean?" I could barely breathe.

"Let's have another opinion on this," he said, avoiding my question and my eyes. "I saw Dr. Brunning here a few minutes ago. She's a neurologist. I'll have her check you out."

Dr. Brunning, a hearty woman, put me through a series of tests to make sure my brain was working properly. She guided me into the hallway and pointed to the tiled floor. Dr. Bashevkin and Reuven stood together, watching.

"Okay, Malia. Try and walk on your tiptoes in a straight line."

"Are you testing me for headaches or for drunken driving?" I asked. I was not feeling in a very jocular mood, but I thought cracking a joke might help me get myself under control and regain my positive outlook. Think positive, I told myself sternly. Don't lose it now.

Dr. Brunning was amused. "I'm glad to see your sense of humor is intact, Malia." She chuckled. "We're just testing your reflexes, Malia. Try touching your finger to your nose . . . Good, that's fine. Now repeat the following words after me . . ."

I dutifully repeated the stream of words, then watched as she banged my elbows and knees to make sure my reflexes responded properly.

"Don't worry, Malia," she told me at last. "Your brain is just fine! Now, let me check your eyes."

She performed the same test Dr. Bashevkin had performed earlier. Then she turned off the bright light and sat back. "Malia, I can't see the entire disc. Dr. Bashevkin was right."

"What does it mean?"

Dr. Brunning paused. "You know, doctors have a tendency to think of the worst possible cause for any symptom."

"And what would the worst be in this case?" I asked quietly.

"If the entire disc can't be seen, that can mean that something from behind is blocking it. That something, whatever it is, can cause pressure against a vein, which might be causing your headache." She paused again. "That something might be a tumor."

A brain tumor! Heaven help me. It couldn't be!

"One way to find out is to perform a CAT scan and MRI, two tests that show us images of the brain," she went on. "But before we subject you to those tests, I think we should have an ophthalmologist take one more look at your eyes."

By now, I would have surely developed a headache, even if I hadn't had one before! Dazed, I followed Dr. Brunning back into the main office at K-8 and waited to find out where to go for an ophthalmologist to check me out. Dr. Bashevkin was still with Reuven, anxiously awaiting the test results. I felt so grateful to him for waiting with us and giving us moral support.

Dr. Bashevkin led us to another building, where Dr. Safra, the ophthalmologist, was expecting me. I received three different kinds of eye drops before he examined me. No one in the room dared breathe.

After a few minutes of unbearable suspense, Dr. Safra looked up from his instruments and smiled. "Absolutely no problem," he announced. "There's no pressure from any veins or anything else in the brain. Young lady, you're doing just fine."

The surge of relief was so strong I would have had to sit down had I not been sitting already. Reuven, too, was laughing with relief, thanking Dr. Bashevkin for his care and concern. Thank Heaven, the headaches were nothing to worry about.

"Okay, now that I know I'm fine," I said, "why do I have these headaches?"

"It's hard to say," said Dr. Bashevkin. "It could be your wisdom tooth, as you suggested. It might also be a reaction to the high dose of chemo you've been receiving. At any rate, you're fine. Let's just give you one more dose of platelets to tide you over the weekend. Then you can come back at the end of next week and see if you're ready to start your next round."

"Can I ask you another question, doctor?"

"Of course. Anything you want to know, just ask."

I fidgeted. "Next Tuesday will be Tishah b'Av, a day of fasting in memory of the destruction of the Temple in Jerusalem two thousand years ago."

He nodded. "I know."

"Well, I would like to fast, but everyone thinks I'm being ridiculous. They think it would be dangerous since I'm on chemotherapy."

"Hm." He stroked his chin. "Is this really important to you?"

"Yes, it really is. Mourning over the loss of the Temple keeps us connected to it. It keeps the Temple alive in our hearts. If I don't fast I won't feel that deep sorrow, and my connection to the Temple will become weaker. Especially at this time in my life, when I'm in such terrible danger, I want that connection to be strong. I don't want it to slip away."

"I understand perfectly," he said. "I really do. Fasting will starve your body but nourish your spirit."

"That's it exactly," I said, relieved that he understood me so well.

"In your case, you can fast, Malia," he said. "We need your spirit strong and healthy to fight this disease. But be smart. If you begin to feel weak or ill in the slightest, break your fast and call me immediately."

By the time we got home that Friday, it was early afternoon. I took a nap, then helped Mother in the kitchen — as much as she let me. I got such pleasure out of doing things for Shabbos. Dov wasn't coming from Monsey for Shabbos, because we'd already made plans to go to Monsey ourselves on Sunday for a few days. I intended to get extra rest on Shabbos so that I would be up to the exertions of the coming week.

It was a typical summer Shabbos in Flatbush, very quiet and peaceful. Much of the neighborhood had emptied out, as people fled to the mountains to escape the hot weather. I didn't mind the heat. I didn't mind anything. I was alive.

Reuven and I arrived in Monsey on Sunday evening. It was wonderful to see Dov's face light up at the sight of me when I got out of the car. He dashed forward to give me a big hug, then ran back to the carriage where Ari was sitting. "Mommy came!" he yelled at his little brother.

I hugged and kissed them tightly, then straightened up, still holding Dov. "Hi," I said to the rest of the Panzers.

It was a marvelous little vacation. I was able to enjoy my children, while my mother-in-law and my sisters-in-law fed, dressed and bathed them. I slept late, ate delicious, healthful meals and played with my children when they came home from day camp.

I fasted on Tishah b'Av, and I was just fine. My mother-in-law fussed over me, asking me anxiously over and over again if I was feeling all right, but I kept assuring her that I was feeling okay. I felt so good when the fast was over and I'd managed to keep it the entire day.

Wednesday was my last day in Monsey with the children. I wanted to make the most of it. My mother-in-law and I took Dov and Ari to Discovery Zone, an indoor amusement park in Monsey. While my mother-in-law watched Ari, Dov and I climbed up blocks, jumped on rubber beams and swam through thousands of colored balls. We didn't stop laughing the entire morning.

We came home to a late lunch and the prospect of a quiet afternoon. But shortly after we'd finished eating, the doorbell rang.

"Could you get the door, Malia?" my mother-in-law said.

I opened the door. There stood Mother and Father, holding a beautiful birthday cake. "Happy birthday, Malia!" they chorused.

I stood there with my mouth open. I couldn't believe it! My English birthday had been the day before, on Tishah b'Av, but it had completely slipped my mind. Both families had planned a surprise birthday party right under my nose, and I hadn't suspected a thing.

It was a wonderful party. We reminisced and talked until late. Dov loved the cake, while Ari enjoyed playing with the balloons. At last, with a great feeling of reluctance, Reuven, Mother, Father and I took our leave of the Panzers. It was time to head back to Flatbush and get ready for my next round of chemotherapy. G-d willing, it would be the last.

The Final Round

Thursday afternoon, I went to Maimonides Hospital for a blood prick. My counts were very high, and I thanked Hashem in my heart.

"This is excellent, Malia," Dr. Bashevkin said with approval. "You'll be able to start chemotherapy tomorrow."

"The last round?" I said hopefully.

"G-d willing. We'll take a bone marrow test afterwards to find out."

With high expectations, we went home and packed up my things, eagerly awaiting the call from the hospital on Friday morning that my bed was ready for me. When Mother, Reuven and I arrived, we found that instead of my usual room, I'd been put into the room right next door to Rose's.

"I'm going over to say hello," I told Mother as she put my things in the locker. "I'll be right back."

Rose's bed was empty. Had she been moved? Released from the hospital? I checked; her little tag was still there. Maybe she was taking a walk.

A nurse I didn't recognize came into the room. She looked at me strangely.

"Excuse me," I said. "Do you know where I can find Rose Scheiner?"

"Are you a relative of hers?" the nurse asked.

I was a little taken aback. "No, I'm a friend. I'm a patient on this floor. I was just admitted." I felt the first trickle of unease creeping down my spine. Anxiously, I asked, "Is she downstairs having surgery?"

"No," the nurse replied. She didn't elaborate.

"Did she go home?"

"No," the nurse said again.

"Well then, where is she?"

The nurse looked straight at me. "She died this morning," she said quietly, then turned and walked away.

I was stunned. Although I had been living with the reality of cancer for months, this was the first time I had come face to face with death. The word shocked and terrified me. But I pushed thoughts of my own mortality from my mind. I would think only positive thoughts. I would hold on to my faith in Hashem. I would keep my spirit strong. Death was not a welcome visitor in my mind.

But what about Rose? Forgetting about myself, I thought of this friend whom I would never see again, and tears trickled down my cheeks. My sense of loss was so strong I could feel it in my stomach. If only I'd come to the hospital just two or three hours earlier, I would have been able to say goodbye. If only. Such a frightening pair of words.

Marcia Gellis saw me coming out of Rose's room, my face wet with tears. "I'm sorry," she said quietly. "I'd hoped you wouldn't find out."

"How did it happen?" I asked.

"I heard them paging 'Code 3' this morning to Room 5819. That means her heart stopped and she wasn't breathing. The doctors came running and did what they could, but . . ." She sighed.

"I guess it was just her time," I said softly.

"I'm sorry," Marcia said again. Then she looked down at the chart in her hand and hurried down the hall.

It was just her time, I thought again as I walked back into the room to tell Mother and Reuven what had happened. When was my time? When was anyone's time? No one ever knew. I hoped she hadn't been in pain when she passed away. I was going to miss her.

Shortly after we'd settled in, Joseline came into the room. She'd been my nurse once before, and she was able to fill in most of my paperwork without asking me any questions. Once we'd gotten that out of the way, she gave me an identification bracelet, ordered an "egg crate" for my bed and asked the IV nurse to come access the infusaport as soon as possible.

Soon after I was started on the chemo, Joseline came in and attached some papers to the empty bed next to mine.

"I'm getting a roommate?" I asked, surprised. Although I was always in a semi-private room, they tried to avoid giving me a roommate, so I wouldn't be exposed to unnecessary germs.

"Yes," Joseline replied. "Don't worry, she doesn't have anything contagious."

My Spanish roommate soon settled into the room. Apparently, she had become addicted to drugs and damaged her stomach. She would be in the hospital for less than a week.

If nothing else, she made our week interesting. Her Spanish-language television shows were on full blast all hours of the day. Whenever she wasn't actually sleeping, she watched television avidly, laughing out loud when she thought something was funny. It was a little annoying at first, but eventually, we found her rather amusing. She fixed her hair in rollers every single night, though why that was necessary in a hospital was beyond me. The night before she left she packed all her things away, including her rollers. But of course, she couldn't go to sleep without rollers in her hair, so she made some out of the cardboard tubes from toilet paper rolls. She always chattered to us in a cheerful mixture of English and Spanish; it didn't seem to matter whether we understood her or not.

The chemotherapy was going well. I felt good. Whenever I wasn't plugged into the chemo machine, I took little walks with Mother. I felt a pang every time I passed Rose's room. A stranger now occupied her bed.

Mother and I had purchased identical robes during the two weeks I was at home. Now, as we strolled down the hall together, we kept hearing comments.

"How sweet! Are you sisters?"

"No," we answered.

"Twins?" another woman tried.

"No, we're mother and daughter!" we said happily. The sparkle in Mother's eyes matched my own.

My roommate called us *hemelas,* which means twins in Spanish. She thought our matching robes were adorable. One nurse, who was from Grenada, saw beyond the identical robes to the special relationship we shared.

"In my country, parents are people to respect and treat with deference," she told us. "Here in America, children are disrespectful and talk back to their parents. It's so nice to see a mother and daughter in this day and age having such a nice relationship."

The remainder of my stay passed smoothly. When I wasn't plugged in, I walked; when I was, I slept. This round was even better than the one before. I actually had a little appetite and managed to eat something at each of the meals. My ears were barely clogged, and my vision was not at all blurry.

Tuesday morning, we packed and prepared to leave. I looked at the familiar halls of G-8. G-d willing, this would be the last time I would be here as a patient. I was so excited I would have danced had I had the strength.

The nurses gave me a rousing, cheerful farewell.

"Next time, we want to see you in the maternity ward!" they told me.

We left the hospital. I took a deep breath of fresh air and looked back at the massive building. I knew I would have to return to K-8 for transfusions, but I hoped and prayed I would not need to come back as a patient.

When we got home, I went straight to bed. I was still very weak and tired, but with each passing hour, I felt my strength returning.

Monday morning, I returned to K-8 as an outpatient for another round of transfusions. Mother and Reuven accompanied me as they had done so many times before. As I waited for a volunteer to bring the blood for my transfusions, I had a cup of hot tea and a danish in the kitchen.

When I finished, I went to sit down on the comfortable recliner where I would receive the transfusions.

"How's Ari doing?" Geula greeted me. "Any teeth yet?"

As always we compared notes about our babies. After chatting for a minute or two, she took my temperature. She turned the thermometer to the light and raised her eyebrows in surprise.

"Malia, did you know you're running a fever?"

"A fever?" I stared at her. "No, of course not. I'm fine!"

"You may feel fine, but this thermometer says you're running 101."

"It can't be," I protested. "Maybe it's because I just drank a cup of hot tea. That could make the thermometer register a fever, couldn't it?"

"It's possible," Geula conceded. "Sit quietly for ten minutes, and then I'll take it again."

Nervously, I sat on the recliner. After the excitement caused by my little headache, I hated to think how they would react to a fever. Ten minutes later, Geula came back to me and took my temperature again. Sure enough, I had a fever. Geula called my doctors. Dr. Kopel came to check me out.

"Sorry, Malia," he said sympathetically. "You'll have to be admitted into the hospital until your fever goes down."

"Oh, no." I exchanged a look of dismay with Reuven and Mother. Who could have possibly expected this?

"Don't worry," Dr. Kopel said kindly. "No need for alarm. It's actually quite common for chemotherapy patients with low white blood counts to come down with fever. You're very lucky you haven't had fever until now. Many patients get fever or other infections between every round of chemotherapy."

I looked at Mother and Reuven again, this time with a rueful smile. There are so many times when a person doesn't even realize the need for gratitude. What a turnaround. Instead of being upset I was running a fever, I should be thankful to Hashem I had avoided a fever until now.

Dr. Kopel called the admissions office. Within half an hour, I was back in G-8 in my regular bed. The nurses were shocked to see me.

"You're not supposed to be back here!" Marcia scolded me.

I pointed at the IV with antibiotics plugged into my infusaport. "It was Dr. Kopel's idea, not mine," I said with a mock scowl.

It seemed strange to be there, with my usual nurses, at a time when I felt well and relatively strong. I hoped I would only need to be hospitalized for a day or two, but on Thursday, I was still feverish. It seemed I was facing another Shabbos in the hospital and, as always, my mother was with me. Reuven went to the house to pack some things for us. I had an overwhelming feeling of déjà vu.

That Friday afternoon, Dr. Shulman and Dr. Shulman came by to visit, as they so often did. They lived very close to the hospital, and they had often invited Mother to come and eat a Shabbos meal with them. Mother had always declined, since she didn't want to leave me alone.

This time, when they extended their usual invitation to Mother, I spoke up before Mother could refuse. "Please go, Mother. I'm not on chemotherapy and I'm feeling just fine."

Mother finally gave in. She left early Shabbos morning, while I was still asleep, to enjoy a rushed but beautiful meal at the Shulmans. When she came back, I was still fast asleep. Motzaei Shabbos, my cousin Devora came to visit, armed with pizza and nosh. We had a spirited little part and invited the nurses to join us.

Soon after Devora left, I had my temperature taken. Thank Heaven, the fever was finally going down.

When Dr. Kopel checked me Sunday morning, he gave me a big smile. "You're doing all right, Malia!" he told me. "I think we'll send you home."

Hopefully, I told myself, this will really, really be my final farewell to the hospital. Reuven and I had decided that, since I was feeling reasonably well, I should recuperate in Monsey in close proximity to my children.

It was a good choice. As always, my mother-in-law took excellent care of me. She served me rib steak and freshly squeezed orange juice in order to help me recover my strength, and she made sure I got enough sleep. I relaxed in the sun and played with my children on the grass, while my mother-in-law and sisters-in-law fed them and took care of them.

How could I ever have recovered so easily without such a marvelous network of support?

The Wedding

The last week in August came. Rachel's wedding was just around the corner. Reuven drove to Monsey to bring my children and me back to Flatbush to stay.

It was a bittersweet farewell. My mother-in-law cried as she hugged and kissed Dov and Ari. For five months, she had been the physical and spiritual "mother" of her grandsons, and now they were going back with us. As for us, there was no way we could ever express our gratitude to her for all she had done for us. I cannot even begin to think what we would have done without her help.

The children made the transition from Monsey to Flatbush very easily. Dov was thrilled to be back home with me, but he did not cling to me too much. He did keep me in sight all the time, however, to make sure I wasn't going anywhere again. Ari, now an active ten-month-old, was pleased to have a new place in which to crawl about.

A week before the wedding, I went to have a bone marrow test taken. It came out clear. Dr. Ruben declared me in remission.

At last! I was in remission! For months and months we had struggled to reach this goal, and now, we were finally there. I was too overwhelmed for words. My eyes brimmed with tears. The doctor,

Mother and Reuven all looked at me, waiting to let me speak first, but there were no words. I closed my eyes and silently thanked Hashem for His kindness. I felt small and unworthy. I knew it was not my merit that had brought about this sweet moment. It was undoubtedly the merit of my parents and my husband, the merit of my ancestors, the merit of my young children who would have been left orphaned if I had died, the merit of the hundreds of people who had sent torrents of prayers heavenward on my behalf. All these had brought me the gift of my life. I was so grateful, and so humbled. Silently, I prayed for the welfare of all my family and friends. I prayed for the Jewish people and all mankind. And I offered up a little prayer for myself. Please, Hashem. Please. Please let me live.

I opened my eyes. Still unable to speak, I simply nodded. Then I wiped away my tears with a tissue my mother gave me.

The doctor cleared his throat to hide his embarrassment. "You'll have to come back in four weeks for another test," he said. "After that, we'll see."

Fortified with the heady knowledge that I was doing so well, I threw myself into the last-minute wedding preparations. Mother and I went out almost daily with the children, shopping and organizing. It was such a pleasure after so many months of only going back and forth from the hospital.

September 8 finally arrived. Rachel's wedding! The house was filled with the excited hustle and bustle of last-minute preparations, a whirlwind of exuberant confusion.

Sarah Daskal, a professional makeup artist, came to our house. Rachel, Mother, and I sat patiently as Sarah expertly applied our makeup for the wedding. She took the longest with me, since I needed false eyelashes and eyebrows as well as makeup. When she finished, I looked in the mirror. I was very pleased. The effect was completely genuine. There was no way anyone could tell they weren't real.

As I got dressed, my mind leaped nervously ahead to the ordeal I knew I would have to face. It would be Rachel's wedding,

but I would also be a focus of attention. Everyone would be looking at me, talking about me, saying in hushed whispers, "She's the
one who . . ."

I lifted my chin. I just wasn't going to care! Hashem had given
me the wonderful gift of life, and I would show my gratitude by letting all the world see my appreciation.

The wedding was beautiful. Rachel was gorgeous in a lovely
satin gown with a full, multi-tiered skirt. When I danced with
her, it seemed to me that she was crowned by an aura far more
glowing than her elegant tiara. Throughout her entire engagement, and even now at her wedding, I was the center of attention. Mother had spent weeks and weeks with me in the hospital instead of shopping and planning with her. Visitors had
inquired about my health and well-being, not about Rachel's
wedding plans. And all that time, the period of her life that was
rightfully hers, Rachel had never shown the slightest bit of
resentment. And I knew that deep down she did not feel any different. I had always been able to tell when she was putting on an
act for the benefit of others. Now was not one of those times.
And on the night of her wedding, her sterling character and selfless love for her sister made her so beautiful in my eyes that it
took my breath away.

All of my doctors were also there. Mother had given all of them
personal invitations to the wedding. They had become such an
integral part of our struggle against leukemia that they were like
family members.

I was very emotional that night. While I spent a great part of the
dancing sitting on the sidelines, I was overjoyed that Hashem had
enabled me to be here, at my sister's wedding. So many people came
over to me to speak to me—doctors, friends, relatives. It was thanks
to their efforts and prayers that I was there.

I finally lost control at the end of the wedding, at the *mitzvah
tantz,* when the *badchan* was singing very movingly about my
parents' devotion to their children. While he didn't say anything

specific, everyone knew he was referring to me and my illness. I
tried to cry quietly, but my eyelashes started falling out one by
one. I felt so embarrassed and tried to avoid letting anyone see,
but my Aunt Shani came to my rescue.

"Look!" she said. "Every tear pulls out an eyelash!"

Maybe it was the way she said it, or maybe it was just the cul-
mination of all the emotional strain, but I burst into hysterical
laughter. Only half my eye had eyelashes at that point, so I pulled
out the rest myself. It didn't matter any more. I was among my loving family, and that was all that mattered.

When life began to go back to normal after all the wedding festivities were over, I still continued to go in for checkups once a
month. The outlook was highly encouraging.

At the end of September, I went to see Dr. Kopel in his new
office, outside the Maimonides complex. My numbers were a
little low.

"Have you had any infections lately?" he asked.

"No." I felt a little nervous. "Is everything okay?"

"Yes, it's fine," he said. "I'm sure they'll go up by next month. I'll
see you at the end of October. Take care of yourself until then."

I had a little extra time, so I went to the Maimonides Blood
Bank. I wanted to thank the staff there for all they had done for me
during the five months I was getting transfusions.

"Hi," I said as I walked in. "My name is Malia Panzer, and I
wanted—"

I was interrupted. "Everyone, look!" the nurse called. "This is
Malia Panzer!"

Many of the staff came crowding around to meet the
young lady for whom so many people had come to donate
blood. I was a little awed by the attention. Is this what the
president feels like, when everyone knows him even though he
doesn't know them?

I thanked them over and over again for their efforts. They
were so nice and friendly. I walked out of the Blood Bank,

proud that here, too, my illness had resulted in bringing such honor to Hashem.

The following month, I went to see Dr. Kopel again. This time my numbers were excellent.

"Your hemoglobin is 14," he said with satisfaction. "That's the best it's been yet."

I was thrilled. "So what do we do now?" I asked eagerly.

He smiled. "I'm going to schedule you for a bone marrow test at the end of November. If that comes out clear, we can take out the infusaport."

I caught my breath. The infusaport, a long-term device, would only come out if the doctors seriously believed I didn't need it any more.

"And if the infusaport does come out?" I asked tentatively. "Do I still have to come in for checkups?"

Dr. Kopel smiled. "Oh, yes, Malia. We like seeing you around here. We'll stretch the time between checkups. It won't have to be every month. But you can be sure we'll be keeping an eye on you for the next few years to make sure you stay in remission. G-d willing, everything will turn out just fine."

I went home and waited impatiently during the next month for my bone marrow test. When I walked into Dr. Ruben's office, it was hard to compare this occasion with that first test he had given me, so long ago, when I'd first gone to the Maimonides emergency room.

I lay on the table for the test. It hurt a little, and I cringed and said, "Ooh!"

Dr. Ruben laughed. "Malia, you're becoming a wimp in your old age!"

I laughed, too. And was eagerly anxious when he called me at home as soon as he got the results.

"You're clear, Malia," he said, his voice exuberant. "You can tell Dr. Kopel to go ahead and have your infusaport removed. You're home free!"

As soon as I hung up the phone, Mother called Dr. Plantilla for me. She told him the good news and arranged for an appointment nine days later to have the infusaport taken out.

Thursday night, December 9, at 5:30 p.m., Mother and I took a car service to Dr. Plantilla's office. We were the first ones there, and we were sent straight into a room.

The nurse gave me a white paper jacket to wear. I had just finished changing when Dr. Plantilla and his assistant came into the room, ready to perform the surgery.

"Hello, Malia." He glanced at Mother. "Mrs. Greenberg, you're not planning on staying during the whole procedure, are you?"

"Why not?" Mother asked.

Dr. Plantilla chuckled. "I don't need two patients!"

He may have been worried about Mother fainting during the operation, but there was no need for concern. Mother, the EMT who had been with me throughout my entire ordeal, was a real pro. She stayed and watched the entire thing.

First, Dr. Plantilla gave me a local anaesthetic in the chest area. Then he cut out the keloid that had formed when the infusaport had first been put in. He remarked, "I told you, Malia, that fair-skinned people often get scars like this. I'm taking it out now, and hopefully, the second cut will heal more cleanly."

"Whatever you say," I said, looking straight at Mother. With the local anaesthetic, I couldn't feel pain, but I definitely felt every yank, pull and pressure. I wasn't sure what was happening, and I didn't have the nerve to look down at what he was doing. I used my over-active imagination instead.

Dr. Plantilla continued the surgery. He made a tiny incision in my skin. As he worked, he gave me a cheerful, running commentary. "I'm making a very small cut, Malia. It heals more nicely. I'm going to locate the five stitches holding the infusaport in place. I also have to find the catheter that leads directly into your vein. It's not so easy to locate it with the small incision. But I don't mind the harder work, and it's better for you."

In middle of the surgery, it started to hurt. I told Dr. Plantilla, and he ordered his assistant to give me more anesthesia. Once the pain faded, I decided to take a peek. I would love to say I'd actually seen surgery being done on me.

I looked down. Augh! I saw opened skin, blood, subcutaneous tissue. I fought back a surge of nausea.

"Is that stuff fat?" I asked weakly.

"Sure is," Dr. Plantilla said cheerfully. "And you hardly have any!" He looked up at my slightly pale face. "I apologize for not working in front of a mirror. Can't see too much at that angle, can you?"

I was grateful to him for helping me relax. I continued to watch the surgery, feeling somewhat like a plucked chicken as he used pliers, scissors and tweezers on me. The assistant was busy applying gauze pads and sponging up blood.

Finally, Dr. Plantilla started to put Humpty Dumpty back together again. He sewed me up with a curved needle and nylon thread. When he'd finished with the stitches, he applied a pressure bandage to secure everything in place.

"You can remove that tomorrow," he said. "You don't have to worry about getting it wet. Do you have Tylenol at home? That's all you'll need in the way of pain relief once the anesthesia wears off." He watched as I touched the bandage gingerly. "Don't worry. You'll be just fine. Come back a week from today, and I'll remove the stitches."

When we were ready, we called Reuven, and he came to pick us up. He settled me gently into the back seat and drove back to the house, where I received royal treatment.

"Are you okay? Would you like an extra pillow? How are you feeling? What can I do to help?"

My entire family is so kind and considerate. My mother-in-law asked to take Ari for the weekend. She didn't offer, she asked—as if I would be doing her a favor. It was a big help, since Ari, who was over a year by now, wouldn't be able to understand that Mommy was tired and couldn't play with him all the time. Dov, on the other hand, considered it a privilege to help take care of me.

As I sat at the kitchen table that night, I noticed Eli's calendar on top of a pile of his books. There was something scribbled in the square for December 9, that day's date. I took a closer look. Eli had written, "Bye-bye, grapefruit!"

I looked at the calendar thoughtfully. Eli must have nick-named my infusaport "grapefruit." Since it was constantly getting poked with needles, it reminded him of the poor grapefruit Mother had used for practice when she first learned how to give me Neupogen shots.

At that moment, when I saw Eli's calendar, I finally realized how much my sickness had become an integral part of the life of every member of my family. Even my youngest brother had this date marked on his calendar. Every relative and every friend had been profoundly affected by my ordeal.

Hashem only gives a ordeal to those who can handle it, I thought. And that includes all those others who are affected indirectly.

I offered up a silent prayer to Hashem that I should continue to be in good health, and that from now on I should bring only hap-piness and joy to everyone around me.

Epilogue

Nearly five years have passed since that fateful day when I first learned of my illness. I cannot say that my ordeal has made me into a different person, because I believe I have always been upbeat and optimistic. But I can say that my ordeal has changed my life. I am no longer a carefree young woman living on a idyllic cloud, oblivious of the sinister side of life, of the suffering and grief that are as much a part of existence in this world as happiness and joy. Never again will a day go by without thoughts of the specter of leukemia. Never again will I experience important occasions without having them colored by my brush with mortality. Never again will there be a day in my life that I will not view as a precious gift from Hashem, a gift for which I am eternally grateful.

Looking back at these past five years, I am overcome by emotion. How incredibly fortunate I've been! My wonderful family and friends were there for me all the time, and that made a world of difference. The doctors and nurses in Maimonides Hospital could not have been more concerned and considerate. The chemotherapy, for all its difficulties, worked for me. I was spared the ordeal of a bone marrow transplant, and I have, *Baruch Hashem* remained clear without any relapses. And the crowning blessing of all: I gave birth to a third son, Meir, three years ago and to my baby daughter, Gila, last year. They are the light and joy of my life. Hashem has been so kind to me, and I am humbled with gratitude.

I have written this book to provide comfort and encouragement to others who find themselves faced with personal crises. It is not my intent to convey the impression that others should expect things to work out for them in same way they did for me. Unfortunately, all too many people have different experiences, and my heart goes out to them. I empathize with them as only someone who has been through a similar ordeal can. Rather, I want to convey the importance of maintaining a positive outlook, of resisting despair, of having faith and trust in the Master of the Universe Who holds the fate of all of us in His hands.

I think that one of the most difficult things about this or any illness is the instinctive sense that we have fallen victim to random events, and that our prospects for recovery are equally dependent on the luck of the draw. We are no longer people but statistics. If this were true, it would be almost impossible to avoid hopelessness and depression. But it is not true. Everything happens by design. Everything we experience is a test, and it is our responsibility to rise to the occasion. We have to find deep within ourselves the courage and tenacity to fight for our lives, but we must do so with dignity and faith. The fight for life should elevate and inspire us and bring us closer to Hashem and the people we love. But whatever happens, we should take comfort in the knowledge that we are in the hands of Hashem. We are not forgotten.

This volume is part of
THE ARTSCROLL SERIES®
an ongoing project of
translations, commentaries and expositions
on Scripture, Mishnah, Talmud, Halachah,
liturgy, history, the classic Rabbinic writings,
biographies and thought.

For a brochure of current publications
visit your local Hebrew bookseller
or contact the publisher:

Mesorah Publications, ltd

4401 Second Avenue
Brooklyn, New York 11232
(718) 921-9000
www.artscroll.com